# MINUTESCRAFT SCIENCE:

# MASTERING TIME FOR LIFE'S SUCCESS

VIVEK KUMAR



BlueRose ONE .com DIY
Stories Matter
NewDelhi • London

BLUEROSE PUBLISHERS
India | U.K.



For permissions requests or inquiries regarding this publication, please contact:

BLUEROSE PUBLISHERS
www.BlueRoseONE.com
info@bluerosepublishers.com
+91 8882 898 898
+4407342408967

ISBN: 978-93-7542-175-7

First Edition: March 2026

*To everyone who has ever whispered,*
*"I wish I had more time..."*
*This book is for you.*
*And to my parents, my family, and the people who believed in me even when my own schedule was chaos—*
*Your love and patience gave me the minutes I needed to become who I am.*

“You don’t just spend time.
You shape your entire life with it, one minute at a time.”
— Vivek Kumar

# Contents

# Foreword

Most of us don't need to be told that time is precious.

We feel it every morning when the alarm rings and our mind starts racing through meetings, messages, and unfinished to-dos. We feel it at night, when another day has slipped by and the things that truly matter still sit at the bottom of the list.

What we *do* need is someone to take us by the hand and say, "You're not broken. Your time system is. Let's fix that—step by step."

That's what this book, **MinutesCraft Science: Mastering Time for Life's Success**, does so well.

From the very first chapter, Vivek Kumar doesn't talk down to you. He doesn't promise some magical 5 a.m. routine that will solve your life. Instead, he explains how time really works in your mind and body—why you feel tired at certain hours, why your focus disappears after too many choices, and why "I don't have time" is often just another way of saying "I haven't decided what matters yet."

He blends science with everyday reality. You'll see terms like *circadian rhythm*, *dopamine*, and *decision fatigue*—but they're wrapped in simple stories: the overworked professional trying to manage emails, the student cramming late into the night, the parent juggling work and home. You don't just read the ideas; you see yourself in them.

**What makes this book stand out is how *practical* it is.**

Vivek doesn't leave you with theory. He gives you tools you can use the same day:

- micro-planning your day into tiny, doable steps
- He introduces the 90-minute focus rule, which aligns with the way your brain functions.
- The two-minute rule helps you overcome procrastination before it escalates.
- This includes time blocking, habit stacking, and establishing small rituals for both mornings and evenings.

There is no pressure to become a superhero.

Instead, there is a gentle, steady invitation:

> Just start with one minute. Then build from there.

You'll also feel something else in these pages—kindness. This is not a book written from a comfortable distance. It's written by someone who has lived the rush, the deadlines, the endless calls, and the guilt of not giving enough time to the things that matter. Vivek brings his years of experience in sales, leadership, coaching, and self-development into a framework that busy people can actually follow.

By the time you reach the later chapters—on the future of time management, deep work, digital overload, and rest—you realize this isn't just about "getting more done." It's about building a life that feels sane, meaningful, and fully lived.

If you are holding this book because you feel constantly behind, overwhelmed, or stuck in patterns you don't like, I have good news:

you're exactly where you need to be.

Read this slowly. Try the exercises. Test the ideas like experiments.

You don't have to change your entire life overnight. You just have to start with the next minute.

Because as this book reminds us, you won't "find" time.

You'll *craft* it—one thoughtful choice at a time.

# Preface

*I didn't write this book because I always managed my time well.*

`I wrote it because, for many years, I didn't.`

I know what it feels like to rush through the day, to live with a constant sense of "I'm late" in your chest. I've been the person juggling work targets, family responsibilities, unread messages, and half-finished dreams—all while telling myself, "I'll sort my life out when things calm down."

But life doesn't calm down on its own.

You and I have to decide how we use our minutes.

**MinutesCraft Science** was born from that realization. Over the years, I've read books, taken courses, coached others, and tested tools in my own hectic schedule. Some ideas worked beautifully. Others sounded good but fell apart in real life. This book is a collection of what actually works—for busy, imperfect, real people.

My goal while writing was simple:

- keep the language easy.
- keep the chapters short.
- keep every idea *usable.*

You'll find science here—about the brain, energy, focus, and habits—but always in simple words and with clear examples. At the end of many chapters, you'll see quick checklists and small actions. They are designed so that even on your most crowded days, you can still make one tiny improvement.

This book is for:

- This book is for working professionals who feel overwhelmed by their daily responsibilities, as well as students who want to study smarter, not just longer.
- This book is for students who want to study more effectively, focusing on smarter strategies rather than just longer hours.
- Entrepreneurs are juggling ten things at once.
- Parents try to balance home, work, and dreams.
- This includes anyone who has ever said, "If only I had more time..."

As you read, don't try to apply everything at once.

Pick one idea from a chapter and test it for a week. Notice what changes. Then add the next one. Think of it like building a house, brick by brick, habit by habit.

If this book helps you reclaim even 30 minutes a day—for your health, your family, or a dream you've postponed—then it has done its job.

Thank you for giving your time to these pages.

I hope they help you give your time back to what truly matters in your life.

# Acknowledgments

No book is a solo effort, and **MinutesCraft Science** is no exception.

First, my heartfelt thanks to my family.

To my parents, who taught me the value of hard work and honesty. I am deeply grateful to my family at home, who have patiently and lovingly accepted my late nights, early mornings, and quiet writing hours. Your support gave me the space to think, write, and rewrite.

To my mentors, managers, and colleagues over the years—you may not know it, but many of the stories and insights in this book were shaped by conversations with you, by challenges we faced together, and by the lessons I learned watching you lead and grow.

To my students, coaching clients, and readers from my earlier books: thank you for your questions, your struggles, and your wins. Seeing you experiment with time management, habits, reading, and personal growth gave me the confidence to put this framework into a book. You are a big reason this work exists.

To the friends who checked in, listened to half-formed ideas, and encouraged me when the manuscript felt too big or too slow—thank you for reminding me to practice what I preach and take one step at a time.

To the editors, designers, and behind-the-scenes professionals who helped shape this into a real book: your careful work turned rough drafts into something clear and readable. I'm deeply grateful for your craft.

And finally, to you—the reader.

```
You chose to spend your precious time with these words. I
don't take that lightly. I hope that something you read here
helps you win back many more minutes, hours, and days for
what you truly care about.
```

Thank you.

# 1

# Introduction: The Science of Every Minute.

"Time isn't just money-it's life itself. Mastering minutes is the art of crafting a meaningful existence."

There are always things to do and not enough time to do them in today's environment. This chapter isn't about packing more into your day; it's about learning how time works, how your brain processes it, and how to utilize that knowledge to spend your time on things that matter. What is the goal? Stop rushing the clock and start working with it. This will make your day feel more planned, balanced, and important.

The truth is that time can't be replaced. You may make more money, get your energy back, and fix broken relationships, but a minute that is lost is gone forever. That's why people who do well usually aren't "busier." They are better at deciding how to spend their time.

Your brain also sees time in a different way. Scrolling for an hour can make the time feel like it has passed, yet focusing deeply for an hour can make the time feel full and rich. It's true that time feels "stretchy"—how you feel, what you're paying attention to, and what you want to do may all influence how you feel about time. Mindfulness can help with this: when you're totally present, time seems to last longer and be more enjoyable.

But mastery isn't only a way of thinking; it's also a way of doing things. People who achieve well don't leave their days to chance. They make them. You will learn how to use: in this chapter.

- Chronobiology to figure out when you have the most energy
- 
- Grouping tasks together to cut down on mental switching
- 
- The 2-Minute Rule to stop putting things off quickly
- 
- Time blocking to keep your mind on one thing
- 
- The 80/20 rule to figure out what's most important

## Why minutes are more important than hours

"One day" doesn't mean that big changes in life happen. They happen with small decisions every minute. A minute of delay can turn into an hour. A minute of action can build momentum.

People also get time wrong all the time: we think things will take less time than they do (planning fallacy) and that "future us" will be very productive (procrastination paradox). Structure, like Pomodoro (25-minute focus sprints), is an easy fix that always increases production compared to work blocks that are sloppy and unplanned.

And that's how habits are formed: by taking small steps. The idea of "tiny habits" by BJ Fogg works because you can do small things over and over again, like reading for one minute, doing two push-ups, or learning five new words. Micro-actions make things more consistent without causing drama.

Find your "minute leaks" first:

checking email all the time

doing more than one thing at once

not sure what to do next

scrolling breaks that weren't planned

It's okay to have some downtime, but mindless downtime is the thief.

**Here are some short tips on the neuroscience of how we perceive time.**

When dopamine levels are high (joy, reward), time flies. It moves slowly when you're bored or stressed. Memory also has something to do with it: new things make stronger memory markers, so life feels "fuller," whereas routine makes weeks blend together.

Take use of that:

add something new to your routines

Chase flow means doing work that is both hard and important.

To slow down the moment, practice mindfulness.

You don't just measure time. Attention shapes it.

## The myth of doing more than one thing at once

Multitasking is mostly task-switching, and it's expensive. Every switch burns mental fuel and creates errors. The fix is monotasking: one task, one window, one finish line.

Helpful tools:

time blocking

"Do Not Disturb" during focus

acting fast when something takes under 2 minutes

Micro-productivity (small steps, big results)

Huge goals feel heavy. Micro-productivity makes them light:

write a book → “write 10 minutes”

learn a language → “5 words”

declutter → “one drawer”

Starting small triggers momentum and makes finishing easier than starting.

**Wrap-up**

Mastering minutes isn’t rigidity—it’s intention. When you understand time perception, stop multitasking, and use micro-actions, you don’t just manage your schedule—you upgrade your life.

```
You won't "find" time. You'll build it-one minute at a time.
```

# 2

# The Myth of Time Scarcity

```
"Time is what we want most, but what we use worst." -
William Penn.
```

We live in a world that loves saying, "There's never enough time." From the second we wake up, it's emails, errands, deadlines, and distractions. But here's the twist: **time scarcity is often more feeling than fact.** The bigger problem usually isn't the 24 hours—it's how we *see* time and how we *use* it. This chapter breaks the "not enough time" myth and shows you how to take your schedule back.

### The illusion of "I don't have time"

"I don't have time" sounds true... But usually it really means, "I **didn't choose this as a priority.**" Everyone gets 24 hours. The difference is allocation.

A simple solution is to track your time before taking action:

```
track your time for 7 days
spot your top 3 time-wasters
replace low-value habits with high-impact work
set -35 priorities max per day
notice how "time pressure" drops when your day has a clear
plan
```

Also: beware the **busyness badge.** Being busy isn't the same as being effective. Real productivity is doing what matters—not doing everything.

### The psychology of time perception

Time isn't experienced equally. An hour waiting feels endless, but an hour doing something you love disappears. That's because your brain measures time through **attention, emotion, and novelty.**

Use this process to your advantage:

```
work in focus blocks (around -6090 minutes)
take short breaks so your brain resets
create "flow" by doing one meaningful task without
interruptions
add a little novelty (new place, new method) when routines
feel dull
```

Another trap: **planning fallacy**—we underestimate how long things take.

A practical fix:

```
use past experience as your baseline
estimate, then multiply by 1.5
add buffer time between tasks
```

Also, stress warps time. When you're anxious, minutes feel heavier.

Simple tools like breathing, gratitude, and short mindful pauses help you reset your internal clock.

```
Time isn't precious only because it's limited--it's precious
because it's your life in motion.
```

### Decision fatigue: the hidden time thief

Every small decision drains mental energy—what to do first, what to reply, what to eat, what to start. That drain adds up. When your brain is tired, you procrastinate, overthink, or choose the easy option instead of the smart one.

Reduce decision fatigue with:

```
routines (same workout time, same planning time)
"decision-free zones" (no heavy choices late at night)
2-minute rule for tiny tasks (do it fast or schedule it)
Eisenhower Matrix (urgent/important filter)
delegate low-impact decisions whenever possible
```

Less deciding = more doing.

### Time blocking: the cure for reactive living

To-do lists are slippery. Time blocking is solid. Instead of hoping you'll "get to it," you give tasks an actual home on your calendar.

Simple ways to make time blocking work:

```
thematic days (one theme per day when possible)
buffer blocks –(2030 minutes between tasks)
no-meeting blocks (protected deep-work time daily)
When your day is blocked, distractions don't run your
schedule--you do.
```

### Rewrite your time narrative.

The words you use about time shape how you live. "I'm too busy" becomes a habit. Swap it for something more honest and empowering:

```
Replace "I don't have time" with "It's not a priority right
now."
treat time like an investment, not an expense
schedule "white space" so your life has breathing room
do weekly time audits
celebrate small "time wins" (finishing early, focused work,
fewer distractions)
```

The myth of time scarcity isn't just inaccurate—it's discouraging. When you stop believing it, you stop living in panic mode… and start living on purpose.

# 3

# The Biology of Productivity.

```
"Your brain is not designed for endless productivity-it's designed for survival. Work with its biology, not against it."
```

## The Brain's Role in Time Management

Your brain is the best at keeping track of time, but it doesn't always work to your advantage. Understanding how your brain functions can enable you to achieve unprecedented levels of productivity. The prefrontal cortex serves as the brain's command center. It makes decisions, maintains focus, and resists any interference. But it also gets fatigued pretty soon. Studies show that people have decision fatigue after only a few hours of intensive mental work. Such fatigue causes them to put off making choices and make unwise ones. This is why planning your hardest tasks for the morning, when your prefrontal brain is fresh, can shift the game.

The brain isn't just logical; it's also incredibly emotional. The limbic system, which governs feelings, often takes over rational planning with thoughts like "I don't want to." This is why willpower isn't enough. Instead, you should make systems that work with the way your brain functions naturally. Habit loops, which are made up of a trigger, a routine, and a reward, make behaviors automatic so you don't have to employ willpower all the time. If you want to go out at 6 AM, get your gym clothes ready the night before (cue), stick to your plan (routine), and have a smoothie after your workout (reward). Over time, your brain learns to want this beat.

Sleep is also very vital. When you sleep deeply, your brain enhances memories and gets rid of metabolic waste, such poisons that can make you lose your mind. Not getting enough sleep makes it harder to focus, be creative, and control your feelings. All of these things are critical for managing your time well. Studies have shown that not getting enough sleep might make you 20% less productive. To get the most out of your brain, you should sleep well for 7 to 9 hours per night and take brief naps (10 to 20 minutes) during the day to recharge.

Neurotransmitters are also highly significant. Dopamine, which is frequently called the "motivation molecule," helps you attain your goals. Serotonin, on the other hand, maintains your mood and focus steady. You can put things off or get burned out if you don't have enough of either. Break your tasks into small wins to boost dopamine. Every time you do a small task, you get a rush of dopamine that keeps you going. Exercise, being outside, and being aware of your thoughts can all help keep your serotonin levels stable.

```
"Your brain isn't supposed to work all the time; it's
supposed to keep you alive." Don't try to change its
biology; work with it.
```

Plan chores that require a lot of focus for the morning. Use habit loops to make things happen automatically. Get between 7 and 9 hours of sleep each night. To receive a burst of dopamine, break things down into small wins. Mindfulness can help keep serotonin levels stable.

## Circadian Rhythms and Peak Performance

Your body runs on a built-in 24-hour clock (your circadian rhythm). When you work *with* it, you feel sharp. When you fight it, you burn out faster. Most people lean toward one of these styles: **Lions** (early peak), **Wolves** (late peak), or **Bears** (middle/9–5). Once you identify your style, you can plan more effectively—engaging in hard thinking when your energy is high and tackling lighter tasks when it dips.

**A few simple wins:**

*Morning sunlight helps you wake up and focus.*

*Less screen/blue light at night helps you sleep better.*

*Room temp matters: cooler for sleep, comfortable-warm for work.*

*Don't eat heavy meals right before bed—it messes with sleep and next-day energy.*

## Focus and distraction (no, it's not "just willpower")

Your attention is limited, and constant pings wreck it. "Multitasking" is really task-switching—and it drains your brain. The fix is **deep work**: one task, no interruptions, for a short block of time. Start with **25 minutes** (Pomodoro), then build up. Turn off notifications, batch emails into set times, and keep your workspace simple—clutter quietly steals focus. Even **10 minutes of mindfulness** a day helps you notice distractions and return to the task faster.

## Energy beats time

You can't add hours to the day, but you *can* upgrade your energy. Think in **90-minute work cycles** with real breaks. Active breaks (walk, stretch, water) refill you; mindless scrolling usually doesn't. Eat in a way that avoids crashes (less sugar spikes, more steady fuel), drink enough water, and move daily—even a short walk can refresh your brain.

## Procrastination is emotional, not laziness

Most procrastination is your brain avoiding discomfort. The best trick is to **start tiny**: open the doc, write one sentence, do two minutes. Momentum does the rest. If perfectionism is the issue, aim for "good enough first draft." Add accountability (tell someone, set a deadline), and reward yourself after finishing a chunk.

## Quick checklist

*Find your chronotype and plan around it*

*Get morning light, cut screens before bed.*

*Do 25-minute focus blocks, batch emails.*

*Work in 90-minute cycles; take active breaks*

## Start tasks with the 2-minute rule

When you understand your brain and body, productivity stops feeling like a fight—and starts feeling like a system.

## Circadian Rhythms and Peak Performance

Your body runs on a 24-hour clock (circadian rhythm). When you work with it, you feel sharp. Fighting it leads to time waste and burnout. Most people fall into one of three types: **lions** (early birds), **wolves** (night owls), and **bears** (somewhere in the middle). Once you know your type, plan your day around your natural energy—don't force yourself into someone else's schedule.

A few simple things make a huge difference:

- **Get morning sunlight** (even 10 minutes) to wake your brain up.
- **Cut screens or blue lights at night** so you sleep better.
- **Keep nights cooler** for sleep, and make your workspace comfort-

able for focus.

- **Stop eating heavy meals late**—it wrecks sleep and next-day energy.

**Focus (the real problem isn't motivation)**

Your focus isn't unlimited. Notifications, multitasking, and constant switching drain your brain fast. The fix is **deep work**: one task, no interruptions. Start with **25-minute focus blocks**, turn off non-essential alerts, batch emails into set times, and keep your workspace clean. Even **10 minutes of mindfulness** a day helps you focus longer.

**Energy beats time**

You can't create more hours, but you *can* raise your energy. Work in **90-minute cycles**, then take real breaks. Walk, stretch, drink water—don't just scroll. Eat steady-fuel foods, stay hydrated, and move daily (even a short walk helps your brain work better).

**Procrastination (it's emotional, not laziness)**

Procrastination is usually your brain avoiding discomfort. The best trick: **start tiny**. Write one sentence. Open the file. Do two minutes. Momentum kicks in. If perfectionism blocks you, aim for "good enough" first. Add accountability, and reward yourself after you finish a chunk.

```
Bottom line: your brain and body aren't the enemy. Once you
understand them, productivity becomes way easier.
```

# 4

# The Power of Micro-Planning.

"You don't have to see the whole staircase; just take the first step."- Martin Luther King Jr.

*Time is the great equalizer. We all get the same 24 hours—yet some people move ahead faster, with less stress. The secret isn't having more time. It's using time differently.*

In this chapter, you'll learn **micro-planning**: a simple, science-backed method of breaking your day into tiny, manageable actions. It turns "too much to do" into a clear next step—so you stop feeling overwhelmed and start building real momentum.

## Why Micro-Planning Works

Here's the truth: **your brain doesn't hate work—it hates big, fuzzy work.**

When a task feels huge and unclear—*write a book, start a business, prepare for exams*—your brain reads it as danger. So you delay. This delay isn't due to laziness but rather a protective mechanism your mind employs to prevent overwhelm.

Micro-planning allows you to change the course of events. Instead of "work on my book," you create a small, clear action like

- "Write for 10 minutes."
- "Outline one section."

Small tasks feel safe and doable. And each small win gives your brain a quick reward—so motivation builds naturally.

Micro-planning also saves mental energy. When you already know the next tiny step, you don't waste time deciding what to do, when to start, or how long it'll take. You just begin.

And once you start? Focus becomes easier. Ten minutes feels manageable. Distractions lose power. Flow comes faster.

**Big progress is usually just small steps done consistently.** Minute by minute, it adds up.

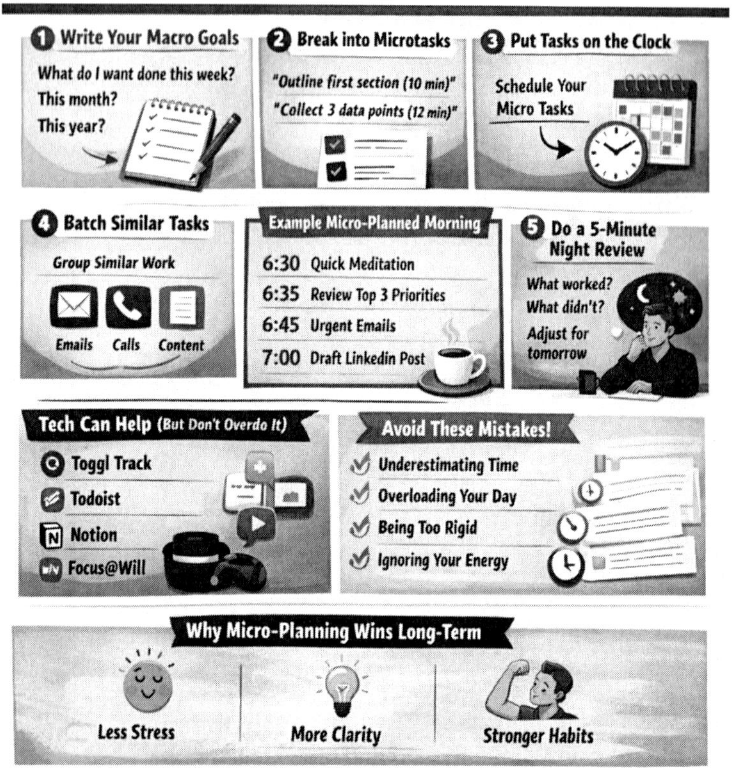


## How to Do Micro-Planning (Without Making It Complicated)

Micro-planning isn't about becoming a robot. It's about stopping the guesswork and giving your day direction.

### *1) Write Your Macro Goals*

Start with the big picture. Ask:

- What do I want done this week?
- This month?
- This year?

Write it down. Clear goals reduce mental clutter.

### *2) Break goals into microtasks.*

Turn every goal into the smallest possible action.
Not: "Write a report."
Instead:

- "Outline first section (10 min)"
- "Collect 3 data points (12 min)"

### *3) Put microtasks on the clock.*

Give each micro-task a real time slot—calendar, planner, notes app—whatever you actually use.

### *4) Batch Similar Tasks*

Group similar work together:

- emails together
- calls together
- content together

Less switching = more progress.

### *5) Do a 5-Minute Night Review*

Before bed, ask:

- What worked today?
- What didn't?
- What will I adjust tomorrow?

That tiny review makes your system smarter every day.

## Example: A Micro-Planned Morning

- **6:30–6:35** — Quick meditation
- **6:35–6:45** — Review top 3 priorities
- **6:45–7:00** — Urgent emails (5 min each)
- **7:00–7:15** — Draft LinkedIn post

No drama. No confusion. You just start.

## Technology Can Help (But Don't Overdo It)

A few simple tools can support micro-planning:

- **Toggl Track** — time tracking
- **Todoist** — subtasks and quick lists
- **Notion** — all-in-one planning
- **Focus@Will** — music for focus sessions

Just don't fall into the trap of "planning as procrastination."

Pick **one or two tools** and keep it moving.

## Common Micro-Planning Mistakes (And Fixes)

**1) Underestimating time**

Track your time for one week, then adjust your estimates.

**2) Overloading your day**

Leave buffer time. Real life will always interrupt.

**3) Being too rigid**

If one block runs long, shift the next block—don't abandon the plan.

**4) Ignoring your energy**

Put challenging tasks in your best hours and lighter tasks in your low-energy window.

**5) Skipping reviews**

Without reflection, you keep repeating the same problems.

## Why Micro-Planning Wins Long-Term

When you micro-plan consistently, you'll notice:

- **less stress**
- **more clarity**
- **stronger habits**
- **steady progress that compounds fast**

Micro-planning is simple:

**Make the next step so small you can't talk yourself out of it.**

Then repeat.

Minute by minute, you stop drifting—and start building the life you want.

# 5

# The 90-Minute Focus Rule.

"The rhythm of the body, the melody of the mind, and the harmony of the soul create the symphony of life."- B.K.S. Iyengar

## The Science Behind Ultradian Rhythms

Your body doesn't run on "hustle mode" all day. It runs on natural cycles of energy and focus. One of the most useful (and most ignored) is the **ultradian rhythm**—basically, your brain works best in **90–120 minute bursts**, then it needs a reset.

Think of it like this: you can usually concentrate hard for about **90 minutes**, and after that your performance starts sliding. You get slower, less creative, and more error-prone. That's not a discipline problem—it's biology.

Athletes already get this. A marathon runner doesn't sprint the whole race—they pace, recover, and repeat. Your brain works the same way. If you take short breaks at the right time, you actually get more done than if you push nonstop.

So here's the simple way to use it:

- Pay attention to when your focus naturally dips (mid-morning, afternoon, etc.).
- When it happens, don't force it—take a **10–20 minute break**.
- Do something that resets you: walk, stretch, breathe, or sit quietly.
- Avoid "fake breaks" like scrolling or checking email—they usually drain you more.

Respecting your ultradian rhythm isn't laziness. It's working smart, the way your brain was designed to work.

By aligning your work sessions with these natural cycles, you'll experience:

- Fewer mental errors
- Higher quality output
- Sustained energy throughout the day
- Reduced stress and burnout

## How to Structure Your 90-Minute Work Blocks

Now that you understand why, let's dive into *how*. A 90-minute focus block isn't just about setting a timer—it's about intentional, distraction-free work. Here's a step-by-step guide:

1. Preparation (5 minutes): Define your goal for the session. What's the single most important task? Clear objectives prevent aimless busywork.
2. Deep Work (90 minutes): Eliminate interruptions. Turn off notifications, close unnecessary tabs, and inform colleagues you're

in a focus session.

3. Recovery (10–20 minutes): Step away from your desk. Physical movement boosts circulation, refreshing your mind.

Take inspiration from author Cal Newport, who champions “deep work” as the key to productivity. He argues that fragmented attention sabotages quality. For instance, a programmer writing code in uninterrupted 90-minute blocks will produce cleaner, more efficient scripts than one constantly switching between tasks.

But what if your job demands constant availability? Negotiate focus windows with your team. For example, schedule “office hours” for meetings and reserve mornings for solo work. Even in chaotic environments, carving out protected time is possible.

```
"Concentration is the secret of strength in politics, in
war, in trade, and, in short, in all management of human
affairs." -- Ralph Waldo Emerson
```

**Common pitfalls to avoid**:

- Multitasking (it fractures attention)
- Skipping breaks (leads to mental fatigue)
- Vague goals (causes procrastination)

## The Role of Recovery in Sustained Productivity

Many believe productivity is about grinding nonstop, but science says otherwise. Recovery isn't optional—it's the fuel for high performance. During breaks, your brain consolidates information, solves subconscious problems, and recharges for the next sprint.

Consider the Pomodoro Technique, which advocates 25-minute work bursts followed by 5-minute breaks. While effective for simple tasks, complex projects benefit more from longer, 90-minute sessions. The extended focus allows for deeper immersion, while the break prevents burnout.

A study at Stanford University found that employees who took regular breaks were 13% more productive. One tech company even implemented "recharge rooms" with nap pods and meditation spaces, resulting in a 20% drop in turnover.

What makes an effective break?

- Movement: A short walk increases blood flow to the brain.
- Mindfulness: Breathing exercises reduce stress hormones.
- Novelty: Switching environments resets your perspective.

```
"Rest is not idleness, and to lie sometimes on the grass
under trees on a summer's day, listening to the murmur of
the water, or watching the clouds float across the sky, is
by no means a waste of time." -- John Lubbock
```

Avoid "pseudo-work" breaks—scrolling social media or reading news. These activities drain mental energy instead of restoring it.

## Real-World Applications: From CEOs to Students

The 90-minute rule isn't theoretical; it's practiced by high achievers across fields.

**Entrepreneurs:** Elon Musk famously divides his day into 5-minute slots, but he clusters similar activities into 90-minute themes (e.g., engineering reviews, executive meetings). This minimizes context-switching.

**Artists:** Composer Ludwig van Beethoven took long walks after intense composing sessions, returning with fresh ideas. His breaks were part of his creative process.

**Students:** Medical students who studied in 90-minute intervals with breaks retained 30% more information than those cramming for hours.

Even in parenting, the rule applies. A parent might focus fully on playing with their child for 90 minutes, then take a break to recharge, leading to more meaningful interactions.

```
"Time isn't the enemy--your misuse of it is." -- Vivek Kumar
```

Key takeaways for different professions:

**Writers:** Draft in 90-minute sprints; edit in shorter sessions.

**Engineers:** Code without interruptions; debug after a break.
**Teachers:** Plan lessons in focused blocks; grade papers in batches.

## Troubleshooting Common Challenges

Adopting the 90-minute rule isn't always seamless. Here's how to overcome obstacles:

**Problem 1: "I get interrupted constantly."**
Solution: Communicate your focus schedule. Use a "do not disturb" sign or status update. Most interruptions aren't emergencies.

**Problem 2: "I can't focus for 90 minutes."**
Solution: Start with shorter sessions (e.g., 45 minutes) and gradually increase. Train your focus like a muscle.

**Problem 3: "Breaks feel unproductive."**
Solution: Reframe breaks as *strategic recovery*, not wasted time. Track how they improve your output.

**Problem 4: "My job is reactive (e.g., customer support)."**
Solution: Batch reactive tasks into designated windows. For example, check emails every two hours instead of constantly.

```
"Discipline is choosing between what you want now and what
you want most."- Abraham Lincoln
```

Final checklist for success:

- Experiment with timing (adjust the 90-minute window if needed).
- Protect your focus blocks like important meetings.
- Measure progress—energy levels, output quality, and stress reduction.

By mastering the 90-minute focus rule, you're not just managing time—you're optimizing your biology for peak performance.

# 6

# The Art of Saying No.

"You can't pour from an empty cup. Saying no isn't rejection--it's self-preservation."

People often view being "busy" as a virtue. But honestly? The real superpower is being able to say **no**.

For a lot of people, "no" feels harsh—like you're letting someone down, missing an opportunity, or proving you're not ambitious enough. But here's the simple truth: **every time you say yes to something that doesn't matter, you're quietly saying no to something that does.** Your goals. Your health. Your peace. Your priorities.

This chapter is about why setting boundaries is difficult, what over-committing secretly costs you, and how to say no in a way that's clear, respectful, and guilt-free. Because once you learn to refuse the right things, you gain back something priceless: **time, energy, focus, and a life that actually fits you.**

**The "Yes" Trap (and why it messes with your life)**

Saying no is hard because most of us grew up chasing approval. We tend to default to saying yes, fearing disappointment, missing out, or appearing selfish. The problem is: **every extra yes creates "time debt."** Your future self ends up paying for it with stress, rushed work, and burnout.

A simple mindset shift helps: **time isn't renewable.** You can earn money again. You can't earn back your hours. So if you don't protect your time, someone else will happily spend it for you.

Quick audit:

- Write down your current "yeses" (work, social, personal)
- Mark them **aligned** (they move you forward) or **misaligned** (they drain you)
- For misaligned ones, ask: *What am I afraid of—guilt, FOMO, conflict?*
- Reframe: **"Saying no to this means saying yes to ___."**

**What happens when you start setting boundaries**

People usually respect you more when you're clear. Boundaries signal confidence and self-awareness. And practically? They protect your focus—because interruptions can wreck your concentration and steal a lot more time than you think.

Easy scripts:

- "I'm on a deadline—can we talk at **3 pm**?"
- "I can't take this on right now, but I can help next month if it's still a priority."
- "I'm not the right person for this—have you tried **[name/resource]**?"

•

**How to say no without guilt**

You can be kind and still say no.

Try these:

1. **The delayed no:** "Let me check and get back to you."
2. **The redirect no:** "I can't lead it, but I can review it."
3. **The values no:** "Weekends are family time for me, so I'll pass."

```
Don't forget: you also need to say no to yourself
```

Some of your biggest time drains are self-made—scrolling, overthinking, perfectionism, and "busywork."

Make a simple "stop-doing" list:

- What eats time but gives nothing back?
- What would I gain if I stopped?
- Replace just one thing each week with a higher-value habit.

**The big point**

**Every no makes space for a better yes.** There will be less resentment, more energy, and more control. And a schedule that finally looks like *your* priorities—not everyone else's.

# 7

# The Pomodoro Technique Re imagined.

*"Time isn't the enemy—it's the canvas. The Pomodoro Technique is your brush. Master the strokes, and you'll paint a masterpiece of productivity."*

The Pomodoro Technique, developed by Francesco Cirillo in the late 1980s, has long been a cornerstone of time management. At its core, it's simple: work for 25 minutes, take a 5-minute break, and repeat. But in today's fast-paced, distraction-filled world, this classic approach needs an upgrade. In this chapter, we'll explore how to reimagine the Pomodoro Technique for modern productivity, blending neuroscience, behavioral psychology, and real-world adaptability to help you maximize every minute.

## The Science Behind the Pomodoro Technique

The Pomodoro Technique works because your brain isn't built for nonstop focus. Most people can concentrate well for **20–30 minutes**, then attention starts slipping. Pomodoro keeps you in short, focused bursts so you don't hit that "fried brain" zone.

But the classic **25/5** isn't magic—it's just a starting point. Different work needs different rhythms:

- **Deep work** (writing, coding, strategy): try **50 minutes on / 10 minutes off**
- **Shallow work** (emails, admin): try **15 minutes on / 3 minutes off**

The real win is that Pomodoro forces **single-tasking**. No multitasking, no bouncing around—because switching tasks kills productivity fast. And it only works if you protect it: silence notifications, close extra tabs, and make your workspace as distraction-free as possible.

Also—breaks matter. Scrolling isn't a break. Better breaks are:

- a quick walk
- stretching
- water
- deep breathing
- one song to reset your mood

```
Bottom line: use Pomodoro like a tool, not a rule. Adjust
the timing to fit the task, take real breaks, and you'll get
more done without feeling drained.
```

# 8

# The Hidden Time Thieves

*"It's not enough to be busy; so are the ants. The question is: What are we busy about?" — Henry David Thoreau.*

## The Illusion of Busyness

We live in a world that treats "busy" like a trophy. If your calendar isn't packed and your phone isn't buzzing, it's like people assume you're not serious. But being busy doesn't automatically mean you're making progress. A lot of "busy" is just **time leaking out in small, sneaky ways**—emails, meetings, multitasking, constant switching.

Think about a typical workday: replying to messages, jumping from call to call, trying to do five things at once. It looks productive from the outside, but inside it's mostly **reacting**, not moving your real priorities forward. And every interruption comes with a cost—once your focus breaks, it takes time to get it back.

Another trap is the "more hours = more results" mindset. Past a point, longer hours don't help—you just get tired, slower, and less creative. That's how burnout happens, and ironically it makes time management worse, not better.

The way out starts with one thing: **awareness**. Track your time for a week—not just what you do, but what drains your mental energy. Then ask yourself: *Is this actually high-impact, or am I just staying busy?* Once you see the patterns, you can start taking your minutes back.

Conduct a time audit for one week

- Identify tasks that feel urgent but aren't important
- Set boundaries to prevent unnecessary interruptions
- Prioritize deep work over shallow tasks
- Reassess your definition of "productive."

## The Myth of Multitasking

Multitasking gets praised like it's a superpower, but honestly, it's mostly a trap. Our brains aren't built to do two demanding things at once. What we call "multitasking" is usually just **task-switching**—bouncing back and forth so fast it feels productive, while your brain quietly gets tired and sloppy.

Think about the last time you tried to write an email during a call. You probably missed part of the conversation, and the email wasn't your best work either. That's because every switch forces your brain to "reload" the task, and that costs energy, time, and accuracy.

The worst part? Multitasking gives you a fake feeling of efficiency. You're busy, but you're not really moving faster—you're just splitting your attention.

The fix is simple: **single-tasking**. Please dedicate your full attention to one important task for a designated period, and you will achieve better results in less time.

Try this:

- Turn off notifications when you're doing deep work
- Use Pomodoro (25 minutes focused, short break)
- Batch similar tasks (reply to messages in one go)
- Practice a little mindfulness to train your attention
- Remind yourself: some tasks deserve your full brain, not half of it.

## Decision Fatigue: The Silent Productivity Killer

Every day, your brain spends energy on tiny choices—what to wear, what to eat, which message to answer first, what task to start. None of it feels heavy in the moment, but it adds up. By the time you hit the decisions that actually matter, you're mentally tired. That's **decision fatigue**—and it's why you can feel "busy" but also weirdly stuck.

That's also why people like Obama and Steve Jobs simplified the small stuff. This is not due to a lack of concern for style, but rather a desire to avoid expending mental energy on insignificant decisions.

You can use the same idea without being extreme:

- **Automate your basics:** fixed morning routine, meal prep, a simple wardrobe, templates for repeat work

- **Make big decisions early:** do the important thinking when your energy is highest
- **Stop overthinking low-impact choices:** decide fast, delegate, or set a default
- **Limit options:** too many choices leads to analysis paralysis
- **Learn from the past:** quick reflection helps you make better calls next time

```
Simple rule: save your brain for the decisions that actually
move your life forward.
```

## The Trap of Perfectionism

Perfectionism is often disguised as a virtue, but in reality, it's one of the most insidious time thieves. Striving for excellence is admirable; refusing to move forward until everything is flawless is a recipe for stagnation. Studies show that perfectionists spend **significantly more time** on tasks than their peers, often with diminishing returns.

Consider the writer who revises a single paragraph for hours, the entrepreneur who delays launching a product until every tiny detail is perfect, or the student who rewrites notes instead of studying new material. Perfectionism doesn't just waste time—it creates anxiety, procrastination, and missed opportunities.

The antidote? **Embrace the 80/20 Rule (Pareto Principle).** Focus on the 20% of effort that yields 80% of results. Ask yourself: "Is this additional time investment truly improving the outcome, or am I just satisfying an unrealistic standard?"

```
"Perfection is not when there is no more to add, but when
there is no more to take away."- Antoine de Saint-Exupéry
```

**Set strict time limits for tasks**

- Define "good enough" before starting
- Seek feedback early instead of over-polishing
- Celebrate progress over perfection
- Practice self-compassion when things aren't flawless

## Digital Distractions: The Modern Time Epidemic-

Our devices were designed to connect us, but they've become one of the greatest threats to our focus. The average person checks their phone **58 times a day**, with many of those interruptions occurring during work hours. Each notification, social media scroll, or "quick" email check fragments our attention, making deep work nearly impossible.

Neuroscience reveals that constant digital interruptions **rewire our brains** to crave instant gratification, reducing our ability to sustain focus. A study by Microsoft found that the human attention span has dropped from 12 seconds in 2000 to just **8 seconds**—shorter than a goldfish's.

Reclaiming your attention starts with **intentional tech use**. Turn off non-essential notifications, schedule designated "distraction windows," and use apps like Freedom or Focus@Will to block temptations. Physical separation—like leaving your phone in another room—can work wonders.

**Enable "Do Not Disturb" during focused work**

- Designate specific times for email/social media
- Use website blockers to limit temptation
- Replace mindless scrolling with mindful breaks
- Audit and unsubscribe from non-essential digital noise

## Conclusion: Reclaiming Your Stolen Minutes

Time thieves don't announce themselves. They slip into our routines unnoticed, disguised as productivity, necessity, or even virtue. But once you recognize them, you can take back control. By eliminating busywork, resisting multitasking, reducing decision fatigue, overcoming perfectionism, and taming digital distractions, you'll unlock hours of previously wasted time.

The key isn't just working harder—it's working smarter.** Every minute you reclaim is a minute you can spend on what truly matters: your goals, your growth, and your joy. Start today. Your future self will thank you.

# 9

# The Role of Rest in Productivity.

"The time to relax is when you don't have time for it."- Sydney J. Harris

## The Myth of Non-Stop Work

For years, hustle culture has sold us this idea: **the more hours you work, the more successful you'll be.** So entrepreneurs brag about sleepless nights, students pull all-nighters, and professionals wear burnout like it's proof they're serious.

But here's the problem: that grind often **kills** productivity instead of boosting it. Rest isn't the enemy of progress—it's what makes progress possible.

Even people we label "workaholics" weren't always grinding nonstop. Thomas Edison, for example, was known for taking short naps and waking up with fresh ideas. And that lines up with what neuroscience shows today: when you step away, your brain keeps working in the background—organizing information, connecting dots, and making problem-solving easier.

Your brain also runs on natural focus-rest cycles called **ultradian rhythms**. You can usually focus strongly for about **90 minutes**, and then your concentration drops. If you push past that point, you don't get "more done"—you get more mistakes, less creativity, and higher stress. That's why the caffeine-fueled marathon often ends with burnout.

So how do we break free from the myth of non-stop work? The first step is recognizing that rest is not wasted time but an investment in sustained productivity. By scheduling deliberate breaks—whether short walks, meditation, or power naps—we allow our brains to reset, leading to sharper focus and better decision-making. The next sections will explore how strategic rest effectively, the science behind sleep's role in performance, and practical ways to integrate rest into even the busiest schedules.

## The Science of Strategic Breaks

Not all breaks actually *refresh* you. A quick scroll on social media feels like a break, but most of the time it just keeps your brain overstimulated. A real break is something that lets your mind shift gears and reset—so you come back sharper, not more drained.

That's why techniques like Pomodoro work: you focus for **25–30 minutes**, then take a short break. Your brain needs those little pauses to process what you're doing in the background. It's also why your best ideas show up in the shower, on a walk, or while you're staring out the window for a minute—your mind finally has space to connect the dots.

Movement helps a lot too. Sitting for hours makes you sluggish, mentally and physically. Even a short walk or a few stretches can wake your brain back up and make it easier to dive in again.

Here are "good break" habits that actually work:

- Take a **5-minute break every 25–30 minutes**
- Do something light: **walk, stretch, move**
- **Avoid screens** during breaks if you can
- Try **deep breathing** or a quick mindful pause
- Use breaks to **drink water** or grab something nourishing

The key is to take breaks deliberately—*before* you're exhausted. Treat them like a non-negotiable appointment with yourself, and your focus (and work quality) will thank you.

## Sleep: The Ultimate Productivity Hack

If breaks are quick pit stops, **sleep is the full reboot**. And in a world that worships busyness, sleep is usually the first thing we cut—ironically, that's what makes us slower, foggier, and more mistake-prone.

Sleep isn't "doing nothing." It's when your brain cleans house, stores memories, and resets your focus and emotions. Skip it, and everything gets harder—decision-making, creativity, even staying calm.

Arianna Huffington learned this the hard way after collapsing from exhaustion. Her takeaway was simple: **you can't run at your best on**

**empty.**

Most adults need **7–9 hours**. And quality matters too. A few basics that actually help:

- keep a consistent sleep/wake time
- wind down with a simple routine (read, breathe, warm shower)
- keep your room cool and dark
- avoid heavy meals and caffeine late
- cut screens/blue light at least an hour before bed

And don't ignore **mental downtime** either. If every spare minute gets filled with scrolling or emails, your brain never gets space to think. A little "white space"—walks, journaling, doing nothing—often leads to your best ideas.

```
Bottom line: rest isn't a reward. It's part of the system.
When you protect it, every waking hour works better.
```

# 10

# The Two-Minute Rule.

"Small disciplines repeated with consistency every day lead to great achievements gained slowly over time."

The Two-Minute Rule That Makes Your Day Feel Lighter

Some mornings, you sit down to work, and you already feel behind.

This isn't due to a lack of motivation. This isn't due to a lack of goals. Instead, it's due to the silent chaos that lurks in the background—small, unfinished tasks.

One example is an email that you neglected to respond to. You intended to file a document. A message you saw and forgot. A plate in the sink. A to-do list full of tiny tasks that don't look serious... until they pile up and start running your life.

And here's the weird part: most of these tasks aren't hard. They're just *small*... and annoying. So we delay them. Then they multiply.

That's why the **Two-Minute Rule** is one of the simplest (and most powerful) tools you can use to get control of your day.

## What Is the Two-Minute Rule?

Productivity expert **David Allen**, in *Getting Things Done*, shared a rule that sounds almost too simple:

**If something takes less than two minutes, do it immediately.**

That's it.

There is no need for a complex system. You don't need to be motivated. There's no need for an elaborate planning system.

Just see **it → do it → move on.**

## Why Small Tasks Feel Heavy

A two-minute task doesn't feel heavy in your hands.

It feels heavy in your head.

When you leave small things undone, your brain keeps them running in the background like open tabs:

- "Reply to that message."
- "Send that confirmation."
- "Pay that bill."
- "Put that file away."
- "Book that appointment."

Individually, they're tiny. But together, they create mental noise. You may not notice it consciously, but it drains focus and increases stress.

It's like carrying a bag filled with small stones. One stone is nothing. Fifty stones? You feel it.

```
The Two-Minute Rule helps you drop those stones before they
become a burden.
```

## The Psychology of Small Wins

The real magic of the Two-Minute Rule is that it creates **momentum**.

When you complete something—no matter how small—your brain gets a quick reward. You feel a little "done" signal. That tiny win makes it easier to take the next step.

And that matters because motivation doesn't always come first.

Most people think it works like this:

**Motivation → Action → Results**

But in real life, it often works like this:

**Action → Momentum → Motivation → Results**

Small wins kickstart that cycle.

## Why We Procrastinate on Small Tasks

People think procrastination is laziness. It's usually not.

We procrastinate on small tasks for very normal reasons:

### *1) "It's not urgent."*

We tell ourselves, *"I'll do it later."*

But "later" doesn't show up. It just becomes another pile.

*2) Starting feels bigger than finishing.*

A task might take 90 seconds, but your brain makes the start feel like a 10-minute chore.

*3) Too many micro-decisions drain you.*

Every unfinished task creates a question:

**Do I do this now or later?**

Those little decisions add up and wear you out.

*4) Unfinished tasks keep nagging your mind.*

Your brain hates open loops. That's why unfinished things keep popping into your thoughts at random times.

The Two-Minute Rule cuts off the debate.

No decision. No delay. Just done.

## What Counts as a Two-Minute Task?

Here are practical examples that fit perfectly:

- replying to a short email or WhatsApp message
- confirming an appointment
- sending a quick "yes/no" response
- filing one document
- putting something back in its place
- wiping a small spill
- washing a cup or plate
- setting a reminder

- paying a quick bill
- making a short call
- forwarding one document
- adding one calendar event

These tiny actions don't look important… but they're the reason your day feels cluttered when they accumulate.

## How to Use the Two-Minute Rule Without Getting Distracted

Here's the one mistake people make: they try to do every two-minute task *instantly*, even during deep work—and then they wonder why they can't focus.

So here's the smarter approach:

### *Use it during "maintenance moments"*

These are perfect times for quick tasks:

- the first 10 minutes of your day
- right after a meeting
- before lunch
- between work blocks
- at the end of the day

That way, you clear clutter *without* breaking your focus.

### *Create a "2-minute list" (your parking lot)*

If you're in deep work and a quick task pops up, don't switch. Just jot it down.

Then handle all those tiny tasks together during your next break.

This keeps you focused and prevents little tasks from piling up in your mind.

## Common Mistakes (So You Don't Ruin a Good System)

### *Mistake #1: "Two minutes" turns into ten*

Be honest with yourself. Some tasks *look* small but expand once you start.

If it's going to take longer, schedule it—don't half-start it.

### *Mistake #2: Doing small tasks to avoid big tasks*

This is the sneaky one.

You answer emails, reorganize folders, tidy your desk… and suddenly the day is over.

You feel busy, but the most important task didn't move.

The Two-Minute Rule is for clearing clutter—not escaping real work.

### *Mistake #3: Perfectionism slows you down*

A quick reply doesn't need to be perfect. It needs to be done.

Progress beats perfection.

## A Simple One-Day Challenge

Try this for **just 24 hours**:

1. Choose one area: **email**, **desk**, or **home chores**
2. Apply the Two-Minute Rule only in that area
3. Notice how your mind feels by the end of the day

Most people are shocked by how much lighter their day feels.

## Action Steps: Micro-Habits for Big Results

✅ **Start your day with 10 minutes of "small wins."**
Clear the tiny tasks first—then start deep work.
✅ **Use the 2-minute parking lot during focus sessions.**
Write tasks down, don't switch.
✅ **Batch quick tasks twice a day.**
Example: 12:30 PM and 5:30 PM.
✅ **Be strict about the time limit.**
If it's more than 2 minutes, schedule it.
✅ **Celebrate the system—not just the results.**
Your identity becomes: *"I handle things immediately."*

## The Ripple Effect of Small Actions

The Two-Minute Rule isn't just a productivity hack. It's a way of living.

It teaches you to stop letting tiny tasks control your mind and steal your time.

It trains you to act instead of delay.

And it creates momentum that spills into bigger goals.

When the minor issues cease to accumulate, you finally find mental and emotional space for what truly matters.

```
Handle the small stuff fast.
 And watch how much smoother life starts to feel.
```

# 11

# The Eisenhower Matrix for Busy Lives.

"What is important is seldom urgent, and what is urgent is seldom important."
- Dwight D. Eisenhower

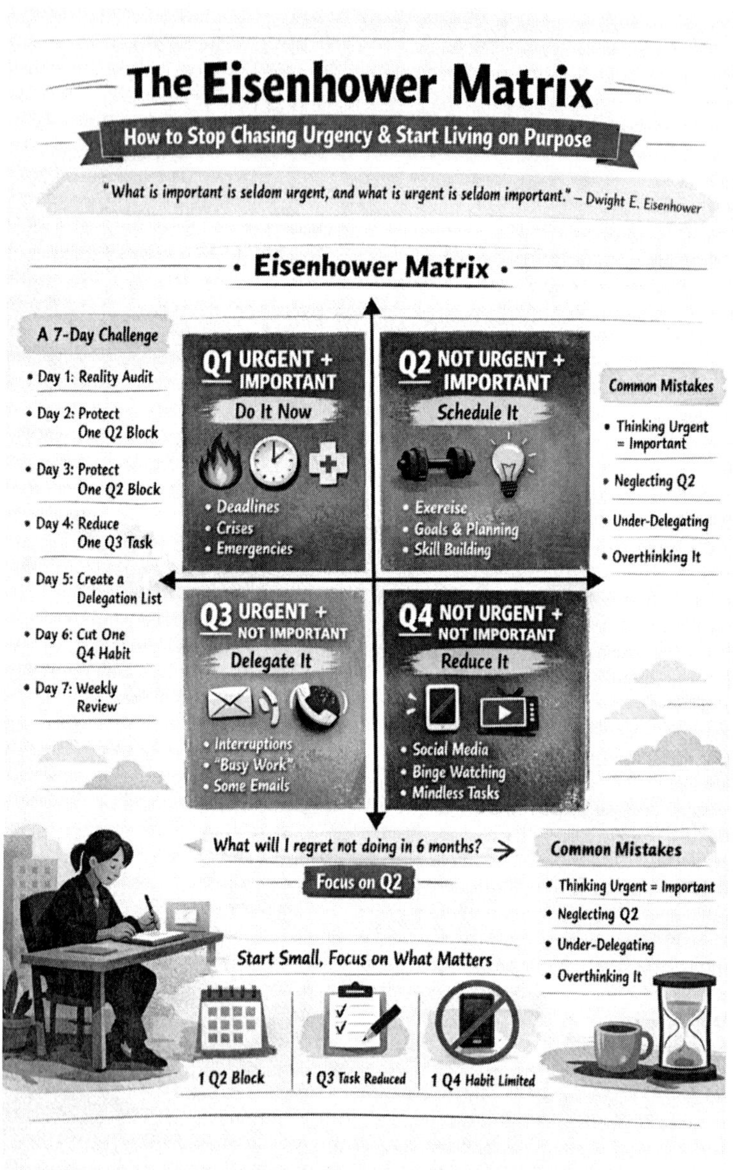
The Eisenhower Matrix
How to Stop Chasing Urgency & Start Living on Purpose
"What is important is seldom urgent, and what is urgent is seldom important." – Dwight E. Eisenhower
• Eisenhower Matrix •
A 7-Day Challenge
• Day 1: Reality Audit
• Day 2: Protect One Q2 Block
• Day 3: Protect One Q2 Block
• Day 4: Reduce One Q3 Task
• Day 5: Create a Delegation List
• Day 6: Cut One Q4 Habit
• Day 7: Weekly Review
Q1 URGENT + IMPORTANT
Do It Now
• Deadlines
• Crises
• Emergencies
Q2 NOT URGENT + IMPORTANT
Schedule It
• Exercise
• Goals & Planning
• Skill Building
Q3 URGENT + NOT IMPORTANT
Delegate It
• Interruptions
• "Busy Work"
• Some Emails
Q4 NOT URGENT + NOT IMPORTANT
Reduce It
• Social Media
• Binge Watching
• Mindless Tasks
Common Mistakes
• Thinking Urgent = Important
• Neglecting Q2
• Under-Delegating
• Overthinking It
What will I regret not doing in 6 months?
Focus on Q2
Start Small, Focus on What Matters
1 Q2 Block
1 Q3 Task Reduced
1 Q4 Habit Limited
Common Mistakes
• Thinking Urgent = Important
• Neglecting Q2
• Under-Delegating
• Overthinking It

In a world where every minute feels like a race against the clock, mastering the art of prioritization is no longer optional—it's essential. The Eisenhower Matrix, named after the 34th U.S. President, who famously balanced military strategy, political leadership, and personal discipline, offers a timeless framework for making deliberate choices about how we spend our time. This chapter will guide you through the science and psychology behind this powerful tool, showing you how to categorize tasks, eliminate distractions, and reclaim control over your schedule. Whether you're a CEO juggling board meetings, a student balancing exams and social life, or an entrepreneur managing a startup, the principles of the Eisenhower Matrix can transform chaos into clarity.

## How to Stop Chasing Urgency and Start Living on Purpose

> *Most people don't struggle with time. They struggle with* ***priorities.*** *Your day doesn't fall apart because you're lazy or disorganized. It falls apart because urgent things shout louder than important things. A message pings. A call comes in. Someone says, "Quick question." And suddenly your whole day is reactive.*

That's why the Eisenhower Matrix works. It gives you a simple way to pause and ask:

**"Is this actually important... or is it just demanding attention?"**

When you start using that question daily, your schedule changes—and so does your stress.

## A Quick Story: The "Busy" Day That Achieves Nothing

Imagine this:

You start your day with good intentions. You plan to work on something meaningful—maybe a project, a report, a book chapter, or skill-building.

Then the day happens.

- You answer emails.
- You jump into meetings.
- You efficiently manage last-minute requests
- You switch tasks all day.

By evening, you're exhausted... But the important thing never moved.

That's the trap: **busy feels productive**, but often it's just *motion without direction.*

The Eisenhower Matrix breaks that cycle.

## What Does the Eisenhower Matrix Really Do?

It sorts your tasks into four simple categories so you stop treating everything like an emergency.

The goal isn't to "do more."

The goal is to spend more time on what actually builds your life and work.

## The Four Quadrants (Simple and Real)

### *Quadrant 1: Urgent + Important*

**Do it now.**

These are real fires. Deadlines. Crises. Emergency problems.

**Examples:**

- a client issue that must be fixed today
- a deadline that can't move
- a health emergency

**Warning:** If you live here every day, burnout is guaranteed.

### *Quadrant 2: Not Urgent + Important*

**Schedule it.**

This is where growth lives—your health, goals, relationships, long-term success.

**Examples:**

- exercise
- writing / deep work
- planning
- learning a skill
- quality family time

**Truth:** If you don't schedule Q2, it won't happen.

### *Quadrant 3: Urgent + Not Important*

**Delegate it.**

This is where a huge amount of time gets wasted. These tasks feel urgent, but they don't move your goals forward.

**Examples:**

- "urgent" emails that don't matter
- unnecessary meetings
- last-minute requests that aren't truly yours
- constant interruptions

**Solution:** Delegate, delay, batch, or politely say no.

### *Quadrant 4: Not Urgent + Not Important*

**Reduce it.**

This is the time-waster zone. Not rest—just mindless draining habits.

**Examples:**

- endless scrolling
- doom-watching
- checking your phone every 5 minutes

**Reminder:** Rest is healthy. Q4 is mostly *escape*.

## The Eisenhower Matrix Worksheet

### *(Use This Today)*

Grab a notebook page and draw a simple 2×2 box.

**Write your tasks under these headings:**

**Q1: Urgent + Important**

**Q2: Not Urgent + Important**

**Q3: Urgent + Not Important**

**Q4: Not Urgent + Not Important**

Now here's the key question:

✅ **What will I regret not doing in 6 months?**

That usually belongs in **Quadrant 2**.

## A Real Example (So It's Easy to Apply)

Let's say you're a working professional:

- Fixing a major customer issue → **Q1**
- Learning a new tool that improves your career → **Q2**
- Responding to random Slack pings → **Q3**
- Scrolling reels for 40 minutes → **Q4**

This matrix doesn't judge you. It just shows you the truth.

## The 7-Day Eisenhower Matrix Challenge

### *(Train Your Brain in One Week)*

You don't need to master this in one day. Just practice it for one week.

### *Day 1: Do a "Reality Audit"*

List everything you did today and label each task Q1–Q4.
**No guilt. Just awareness.**

### *Day 2: Protect One Quadrant 2 Block*

Schedule **one 30-minute Q2 block**.
Examples:

- planning
- writing
- exercise
- skill-building

Treat it like a meeting you can't cancel.

### *Day 3: Find One Quadrant 3 Task to Reduce*

Pick one "urgent but not important" task and reduce it.
Examples:

- batch emails twice daily
- decline one unnecessary meeting
- stop responding instantly to every ping

### *Day 4: Create a "Delegation List"*

Write down 3 tasks you can:

- delegate

- automate
- outsource
- or simply stop doing

Even small delegation frees huge mental energy.

### *Day 5: Cut One Quadrant 4 Habit*

Choose one time-waster and limit it.
Example:

- set a 20-minute timer
- or move social media to one fixed slot daily

### *Day 6: Build a "Q2 Morning"*

Start your day with the most important thing before the world interrupts.
Even **20 minutes** counts.

### *Day 7: Weekly Review (The Secret Weapon)*

Ask yourself:

- What pulled me into Q1 this week?
- What Q3 tasks stole my time?
- What Q2 activity made me feel proud?
- What will I schedule next week?

This is how the system becomes a lifestyle.

## Common Mistakes (And How to Avoid Them)

### *Mistake 1: Thinking every urgent thing is important*

Urgent just means "loud."

Important means "meaningful."

Train yourself to pause before reacting.

### *Mistake 2: Neglecting Quadrant 2*

This is where people lose the most.

Ignore Q2 long enough and it turns into future Q1 crises.

### *Mistake 3: Under-delegating*

Perfectionism is expensive.

If someone else can do it 80% as well, delegate it.

### *Mistake 4: Overthinking the matrix*

Don't aim for perfect labeling.

Aim for better choices.

## Closing: The Real Payoff

The Eisenhower Matrix is not about squeezing more work into your day.

It's about living a life where your time reflects your priorities.

Because the truth is:

**If you don't decide what matters, everything else will decide for you.**

So start small:

- **One Q2 block this week**
- **One Q3 task reduced**
- **One Q4 habit limited**

That's enough to feel the shift.
And once you feel it... you'll never want to go back to "busy" again.

# 12

# The Science of Habit Stacking

"You do not rise to the level of your goals. You fall to the level of your systems."- James Clear

Habit Stacking
How to Make New Habits Stick by Adding Them to Things You Already Do
Attach a New Habit to One You Already Do
Old Habit + = New Habit +
Strong Routine → Bigger Results
Stack Small Habits Into a Simple Routine
WAKE UP
Fresh Start
DRINK WATER
Mobility Habit
WRITE TOP
Planing Habit
READ 5 PAGES
Learning Habit
WAKE UP
Drink Water
STRETCH
For 2 Minutes
WRITE TOP
3 Priorities
READ
5 PAGES
DRINK WATER
STRETCH
PLAN TOP 3
READ 5 PAGES
"You don't rise to the level of your goals. You fall to the level of your systems."
—James Clear, Author of Atomic Habits
Small Steps → Systems → → Better Results
Start Small → Make It a Habit → Level Up
"You don't rise to the level of your goals. You fall to the level of your systems."
— James Clear, Author of Atomic Habits

Habit stacking is basically the "easy mode" way to build new habits.

You add small new actions onto things you already do every day instead of trying to completely change your life overnight (which often leads to burning out in a week). Your brain loves patterns, so when you attach a new habit to an existing one, it sticks faster.

For example, you already brush your teeth every morning. That's a solid habit. Now you "stack" something right after it—like **10 push-ups** or **2 minutes of stretching**. Over time, your brain starts treating them like one single routine: *brush teeth → stretch*. You don't need to think about it further.

What's the best part? Habit stacking doesn't rely on willpower. Willpower runs out. Systems don't. So, instead of waiting to feel motivated, you build a simple chain of actions that happens automatically.

```
Here's what a stacked morning could look like (quick and
realistic):
Wake up and drink a glass of water.
After water, stretch for 2 minutes
After stretching, write your top 3 priorities
After that, read five pages.
```

Each step is small, but together they create a routine that makes your whole day feel more focused and in control.

**The neuroscience behind habit stacking (in plain language)**

Habit stacking works because your brain loves routines. Once you repeat something enough times—like brushing your teeth or making coffee—your brain stores it in a part called the **basal ganglia**, which handles automatic behaviors. That's why you can tie your shoes or drive a familiar route without thinking too hard. Your brain is basically saying, *"Great, I've got this. Let's run it on autopilot."*

Habit stacking takes advantage of that autopilot.

Instead of trying to force a brand-new habit from scratch (which takes effort and willpower), you **attach the new habit to an old one**—like hooking a train car to an engine that's already moving.

Example:

If you make coffee every morning, you can stack something small while it brews—like **two minutes of meditation**, or **writing your top three priorities**. Because the coffee routine is already locked in, the new habit has a much easier entry point.

A great trick here is the **"after X, I will do Y"** plan:

- "After I pour my coffee, I will meditate for two minutes."
- "After I brush my teeth, I will do 10 squats."

That kind of clear cue makes the habit feel more automatic over time.

And there's another bonus: **mini-wins create motivation.** Each small habit you complete gives your brain a tiny reward signal (dopamine). Stack a few easy wins together and you'll feel more energized and consistent—especially with habits you usually procrastinate on.

## How to build your own habit stack

Here's a simple way to create a stack that actually sticks:

### *1) Pick an "anchor" habit you already do daily*

Examples: brushing teeth, morning tea/coffee, lunch, commuting, showering.

### *2) Add one small new habit that fits naturally*

Keep it simple and realistic. Small beats perfect.

### *3) Make it so easy you can't say no*

One page. Two minutes. Five push-ups. Tiny is the secret.

### *4) Use a clear trigger sentence*

"After I _____, I will _____."

### *5) Track it (even casually)*

A checklist or habit tracker helps you stay consistent.

**Example stack (lunch break):**

- After lunch → **10-minute walk**
- While walking → **listen to a podcast**
- After returning → **write one takeaway**

That's not a huge lifestyle change. It's just a smarter version of what you already do.

## Common mistakes (and how to fix them)

**1) Adding too much at once**

Start with **1–2 habits**, not five. Build the chain slowly.

**2) Choosing a bad trigger**

If the anchor habit isn't consistent, the stack won't be either. Pick something you *never miss.*

**3) No reward or satisfaction**

Make it enjoyable—nice music, good tea, a checkmark on a tracker. Small rewards matter.

**4) Doing it at random times**

Stacks work best when they happen in the same situation every day.

If your stack isn't sticking, don't blame yourself—just simplify it and adjust the trigger.

## Advanced habit stacking (when you're ready)

Once your first stack feels automatic, you can build more:

- **Theme stacks:** "morning energy stack," "evening wind-down stack"
- **Social stacks:** do it with a friend or coworker for accountability
- **Layer slowly:** add one new habit only after the previous one feels easy

```
As Robert Collier said: success is small efforts repeated
daily.
 Start small, stack smart, and let momentum do the heavy
 lifting.
```

# 13

# The Magic of Morning Routines.

"The first hour of the morning is the rudder of the day." - Henry Ward Beecher

## The Science Behind a Powerful Morning-

The way you start your morning really does shape the rest of your day. This is not in the clichéd sense of "wake up at 5 AM and your life will change," but rather in a practical, brain-based manner.

When you wake up, your body gets a natural alertness boost. Your mind is usually at its sharpest in those first couple of hours, which is why mornings are a great time for anything that needs focus—planning, writing, studying, problem-solving. If you use that window well, the whole day feels easier.

Mornings also have this "domino effect." When you start with a few small intentional actions—like making your bed, drinking water, or writing your top priorities—your brain registers that as a win. And those small wins create momentum. You feel more in control, more motivated, and less likely to drift into chaos.

But when your morning is rushed and messy, it drains you early. You make a hundred tiny decisions before you've even started your real work, and by midday you're already tired and overwhelmed.

So the takeaway is simple: **a calm, intentional morning doesn't just feel good—it sets the tone for everything that comes after.**

Consider the routines of highly successful individuals:

- Tim Cook (Apple CEO) wakes up at 3:45 AM to review emails and exercise.
- Oprah Winfrey starts her day with meditation and gratitude journaling.
- Before meetings, Elon Musk devotes his first hour to critical thinking exercises.

These routines aren't arbitrary; they're designed to maximize mental clarity and discipline. What is the key takeaway from this? Your morning routine doesn't have to mirror theirs, but it should align with your personal goals and energy cycles.

## Crafting Your Ideal Morning Routine

A powerful morning routine is personal, purposeful, and flexible. It'suit your lifestyle while pushing you toward long-term success. Here's a step-by-step guide to designing one:

- Assess Your Natural Rhythms
- Define Your Non-Negotiables
- Eliminate Decision Fatigue
- Incorporate Mindfulness
- Start Small and Scale Up

## Common Morning Routine Pitfalls (And How to Avoid Them)

Without awareness of these traps, even the most well-laid plans can unravel.

**1. The Snooze Button Sabotage**

Hitting snooze disrupts your sleep cycle, leaving you groggier than if you'd gotten up immediately. The fragmented sleep from multiple alarms tricks your brain into expecting more rest, worsening fatigue. Solution? Place your alarm across the room so you have to physically get up to turn it off.

**2. Digital Overload**

Checking emails or social media first floods your brain with cortisol and dopamine spikes, hijacking your focus. Instead, give yourself at least 30 minutes of screen-free time to center your thoughts.

**3. Overambitious planning.**

Stacking too many activities—like an hour of exercise, 30 minutes of reading, and meal prepping—can lead to burnout. Prioritize quality over quantity.

**4. Neglecting Fuel**

Skipping breakfast or relying on caffeine alone crashes your energy by mid-morning. Opt for protein-rich foods (eggs, Greek yogurt) to sustain mental clarity.

**5. Rigidity**

Life happens. If you miss a workout or oversleep, avoid self-criticism. Adapt and refocus instead of abandoning the entire routine.

## The Role of Rituals in Long-Term Success

Rituals—repetitive, symbolic actions—transform routines from mundane tasks into meaningful practices. Consider the difference between "drinking coffee" and "savoring a quiet moment with your favorite blend while visualizing your goals." The latter engages your senses and emotions, reinforcing commitment to your day.

Athletes often use pre-game rituals to enter a state of "flow." Similarly, a morning ritual signals to your brain that it's time to shift into productivity mode. Examples:

- Lighting a candle to create a calm ambiance
- Reciting affirmations to boost confidence
- Playing an energizing playlist to elevate mood

Research from the *Journal of Experimental Social Psychology* shows that rituals reduce anxiety and enhance performance by providing a sense of control. The more you associate your morning actions with positivity, the more automatic—and rewarding—they become.

## Measuring and Optimizing Your Routine

A successful routine evolves. Track these metrics to refine yours:

**Energy Levels**

Rate your focus and vitality on a scale of 1–10 each day. Notice patterns: Do you crash after certain tasks? Adjust accordingly.

**Task Completion**

Are you consistently achieving your top priorities? If not, reassess your morning planning session.

**Emotional State**

Journaling can reveal whether your routine reduces stress or adds pressure.

**Long-Term Progress**

Every month, review how your routine has impacted your goals. Celebrate wins and iterate.

"You'll never change your life until you change something you do daily."- John C. Maxwell

By treating your morning as sacred, you craft not just a productive day but a purposeful life. Start tomorrow with intention, and watch the minutes transform into momentum.

# 14

# The Evening Wind-Down Ritual.

"A disciplined evening is the foundation of a victorious morning."

## The Science of Unwinding: Why Your Evening Routine Matters

How you end your day is just as important as how you start it. Think about it: your brain doesn't turn off like a lamp. It needs a landing, which is a time to settle down, think about the day, and get ready for bed. If you go directly from stress and devices to bed, you're practically telling your brain to go to sleep while it's still working hard.

That's why a simple nighttime routine can make a big difference. A quiet wind-down helps your brain rest, makes you sleep better, and makes the next day feel smoother—more concentrated and less fragmented.

Priya, a corporate lawyer, is a wonderful example. She used to lie awake at night and had a hard time getting up in the morning. She began conducting a regular 60-minute wind-down with no work emails, no scrolling, and no intensive TV. She started by stretching, writing in a journal, and drinking herbal tea. Within a few weeks, she was sleeping better and feeling brighter during critical talks. Just a simple message to her brain: we're done for the day.

This transformation is what happens behind the scenes: your brain automatically goes from "active mode" to "calm mode" at night, but it needs the correct conditions to do it. Reading, meditating, taking a warm bath, or listening to soft music can all assist that change in happening more quickly. On the other hand, social media and exciting entertainment keep your mind busy and postpone sleep hormones.

The true key is to be consistent. If you do the same relaxing routine most evenings, your body will start to recognize it and say, "Okay, it's time for bed." That's when it's simpler to fall asleep, sleep longer, and feel better when you wake up.

To craft your ideal wind-down ritual, start by auditing your current habits. Ask yourself:

- Do I feel physically and mentally relaxed before bed?
- Am I giving my brain time to detach from work or stressors?
- Are my pre-sleep activities supporting or sabotaging my rest?

The goal isn't perfection but progression. Even small changes—like dimming lights 90 minutes before bed or swapping news podcasts for ambient music—can yield dramatic improvements in sleep quality and next-day energy.

## The Digital Detox: Reclaiming Your Evenings from Screens

In the evenings, a lot of us don't really "log off." We finish dinner… and then slip into hours of screens—scrolling, watching, replying, checking "just one" email. The problem is, your brain doesn't see that as harmless downtime. It reads the light and stimulation as a signal to stay switched on.

Blue light from phones and tablets can mess with melatonin (the sleep hormone), basically tricking your brain into thinking it's still daytime. So even if you're worn out, sleep gets delayed—and the quality drops too.

Take Rohan, a startup founder who used to review reports on his tablet until midnight. He tried a simple rule: **no screens after 9 PM**. Within a couple of weeks, his sleep improved a lot. The big change wasn't just removing screens—it was what he replaced them with: sketching ideas on paper, playing chess with his spouse, and listening to audiobooks without staring at a glowing screen.

If you want to try a digital detox without going extreme, here's a realistic way to do it:

1. **Set a screen curfew**
2. Start small. Move your cutoff earlier by 15 minutes every few days until it feels doable.
3. **Use night mode if you must use a device**
4. Turn on blue-light filters (Night Shift, f.lux, etc.) a couple hours before bed. It's not perfect, but it helps.

5. **Charge your phone outside the bedroom**
6. This one's huge. If your phone isn't next to your pillow, you're way less likely to fall into late-night scrolling.

A simple truth: **the most productive people don't just manage their time—they protect their downtime.**

And it's not only about sleep. When you unplug at night, you get something back that screens quietly steal—calm, creativity, and real connection.

**The power of reflective journaling**

A lot of stress doesn't come from what happened today—it comes from what's still *spinning in your head* when the day ends. That's why journaling at night works so well. When you write, your brain finally gets a chance to process the leftovers: the worries, the wins, the lessons, the stuff you didn't say, and the stuff you still need to do. It's like clearing open tabs before you sleep.

Even 10 minutes is enough. You're not writing a novel—you're just giving your mind a place to unload and sort.

A simple way to do it is the **Three G's**:

- **Gratitude:** three small things you appreciated today.
- **Growth:** 1 thing that didn't go great + what it taught you
- **Goals:** your top three priorities for tomorrow.

That mix is powerful because it keeps you grounded (gratitude), honest (growth), and focused (goals).

And if you hate writing, no problem. Do it in bullet points or record a quick voice note. The point is consistency, not perfection. Over time, journaling starts showing you patterns—what drains you, what energizes you, what you keep avoiding, and what actually makes your days better.

One bonus trick: add a quick **brain dump** page. Just spill every lingering thought—“call plumber,” “pay bill,” “Bali trip idea”—so it stops bouncing around in your mind at midnight.

## The 15-minute “future self” ritual (prep tonight, win tomorrow)

Here’s a simple truth: mornings feel chaotic when you make too many decisions too early. A short prep routine at night gives your “tomorrow self” a head start.

In 15 minutes or less, do this:

1. **Check tomorrow’s calendar**
2. What’s happening? What’s the one thing that would make tomorrow a win?
3. **Set up your basics**
4. Outfit ready. Bag packed. Lunch prepped. Anything that reduces morning friction.
5. **Choose your first action**
6. Make it obvious. Put the materials for your most important task where you’ll see them first thing.

This works because you’re not relying on willpower in the morning—you’re creating a clear runway. You wake up and start, instead of figuring it out.

```
Tomorrow's performance is heavily influenced by tonight's
preparation.
```

## Sleep optimization checklist (keep it simple)

Sleep is the real productivity hack. If sleep is off, everything feels harder—focus, mood, self-control, and energy.

A few basics that make the biggest difference:

- **Cool room** (sleep loves cool air)
- **Dim lights at night** (signals "wind down")
- **Avoid heavy meals late**
- **Light movement** helps (stretch, short walk)
- **Simple breathing** (like 4–7–8) to calm your system

The key isn't perfection—it's consistency. The more predictable your evenings are, the easier sleep becomes.

```
Final thought
Your evening routine isn't just "how you end the day." It's
how you set up your energy, focus, and resilience for
tomorrow. Your best days don't start in the morning--they
start the night before.
```

# 15

# The Digital Detox Strategy.

## The Hidden Cost of Digital Overload

These days, a "digital detox" isn't some fancy wellness trend—it's basic survival. Screens are everywhere: phone, laptop, TV, tablet... And most of us don't even notice how much time we're spending on them until we're suddenly exhausted, distracted, and somehow still behind.

The real damage isn't just the hours. It's what constant digital noise does to your focus. Every notification, every quick scroll, every "let me just check" breaks your attention into tiny pieces. And once your focus is broken, it takes time to get it back. That's why a simple task can take twice as long when your phone is lighting up next to you.

And no, it's not multitasking—it's task-switching. Your brain keeps jumping lanes, paying a mental "switching fee" every time. By the end of the day, you feel busy... but not satisfied.

A digital detox doesn't mean throwing your phone into a river. It's just about putting technology back in its place—**as a tool, not your boss.** Even small rules can change everything. Like Sarah, a marketing executive who tried one simple habit: **no screens before breakfast.** Within a few weeks, her mornings felt calmer, her mind felt clearer, and she got important work done before the day's chaos kicked in.

There's also the emotional side. Too much screen time doesn't just steal productivity—it messes with sleep, increases anxiety, and trains your brain to crave constant stimulation. Late-night scrolling is especially brutal because screens keep your brain "awake," and the blue light makes it harder to wind down. But beyond sleep, the bigger issue is that apps are designed for one thing: **to keep you hooked.** Quick dopamine hits—likes, messages, updates—teach your brain to chase tiny rewards instead of real progress.

That's why so many high performers protect screen-free time. Not because they're "better," but because they're intentional. They create quiet space to think, plan, and actually do deep work—the kind that moves life forward.

If you want to start, keep it simple:

- Notice how often you check your phone in a day
- Identify the apps that drain you the most
- Pick one boundary to try this week (like no screens before breakfast, or no phone in bed)

Because once you disconnect from the noise—even a little—you reconnect with something way more valuable: your focus, your peace, and the things that actually matter.

## The Science of Unplugging: How Detox Boosts Productivity

The benefits of a digital detox aren't just "feel-good" stories—there's real brain science behind why it works.

When you're constantly bouncing between notifications, emails, and endless scrolling, your brain stays stuck in this always-on, slightly stressed state. Over time, this constant bouncing between notifications, emails, and endless scrolling erodes your ability to focus, make sound decisions, and persist in tasks requiring deep thought. Unplugging—even for short stretches—gives your mind a chance to reset. Think of it like rebooting a laptop that's been running 47 tabs all day: once you close the noise, everything runs smoother.

**Why your brain feels better when you unplug**

When screens are nonstop, your attention gets fragmented. You're not doing one thing—you're doing one thing *plus* checking five other things. That constant switching comes with a mental cost. You feel busy, but your brain is worn out.

A detox helps because it reduces the "hyper-stimulation" and gives your focus muscles a break. And the best part is you don't have to quit technology to get the benefits. You just need boundaries.

**The key isn't "no screens" — it's better replacements**

One of the biggest reasons detoxing works is what you replace screen time with. If your break is more scrolling, your brain doesn't really recover—it just gets different stimulation.

But if you replace screens with something that uses your senses—walking, cooking, drawing, journaling, even sitting quietly—your mind resets faster. Nature is especially powerful here. A short walk without your phone can do more for your focus than 15 minutes of social media ever will.

**Sleep improves fast (and it changes everything)**

This is where people experience the results quickly. Late-night screen time doesn't just delay sleep—it keeps your brain mentally "activated." Even if your eyes are tired, your mind stays awake because it's still reacting to information: news, messages, work emails, social drama, random content.

A simple experiment that works for most people:

**no screens 60–90 minutes before bed for one week.**

You'll usually fall asleep faster, sleep deeper, and wake up less groggy. And once sleep improves, everything else gets easier—mood, energy, patience, memory, and motivation.

### *It also makes you more present with people*

Another underrated effect: screens change the *quality* of your conversations. Even when the phone isn't in your hand, just having it nearby can create this subtle "half attention" feeling—like you're not fully there.

That's why simple habits like **no phones at the dinner table** or a **phone basket** at home can improve connection quickly. People feel it. They notice you're more present.

### *Productivity compounds when you reduce digital clutter*

Detoxing doesn't just give you time back—it gives you *mental bandwidth* back. Less noise means:

- fewer mistakes
- faster completion
- better thinking
- less stress

And a huge part of it comes down to tiny shifts like

- turning off non-essential notifications
- checking email at set times instead of all day
- deleting apps you don't even enjoy
- unsubscribing from junk that constantly pulls your attention

## Practical steps for a digital detox that actually sticks

1) **Spot your "trigger moments."**
When do you reach for your phone automatically?

- right after waking up
- between meetings
- when you feel bored or anxious
- during awkward silences
- before sleep

Once you notice your pattern, you can change it.

2) **Swap the habit (don't just remove it)**
If your brain grabs your phone out of habit, give it a replacement:

- keep a book or journal by your bed
- do 10 deep breaths during downtime
- take a short walk without your phone
- stretch for 2 minutes

The goal is: **different default behavior**.

3) **Try "screen sabbath" blocks**
Start small and realistic:

- 30 minutes after lunch
- the first hour after waking
- Sunday morning
- the last hour before bed

Make it easy enough that you'll actually do it.

4) **Put your phone in the wrong place**
This is simple but powerful:

- Charge your phone outside your bedroom.
- Use a simple alarm clock
- Keep your phone in a different room during deep work.

Your environment shapes your habits more than motivation does.

5) **Clean up social media (so it stops owning you)**

- unfollow what drains you
- turn off push notifications
- set one specific time window for social media

- stop passive scrolling—if you're there, engage intentionally

6) **Add accountability**

Tell a friend. Do it with a "detox buddy." Even a simple shared challenge makes it easier to stick.

## The long-term win: deep attention comes back

Over time, the biggest reward of a digital-light lifestyle is this: you get your deep focus back.

You can read longer. Work longer without drifting. Think more clearly. Feel calmer. And your relationships improve because you're actually *there*.

And you don't have to become anti-technology. The goal isn't to live like it's 1995. It's to live like **you're in control**, not your screen.

If you want, I can turn this into a polished **book chapter format** (with headings, a short opening story, and a "7-day digital detox challenge" at the end).

# 16

# The Power of Single-Tasking.

"Multitasking is merely the opportunity to screw up more than one thing at a time."- Steve Uzzell

## The Myth of Multitasking

For years, multitasking has been sold as the ultimate productivity flex—like if you can juggle enough things at once, you're automatically more capable. And yeah, it *sounds* efficient. But in real life, multitasking usually means you're doing several things... **badly**.

Your brain can't truly focus on two demanding tasks at the same time. What it actually does is **switch**—fast. Email... podcast... to-do list... back to email... and every switch costs you time and mental energy. That's why multitasking doesn't just slow you down—it also lowers the quality of what you produce.

Think about the last time you tried to write an email while listening to something and checking your task list. You probably missed parts of what you were listening to, and your email needed extra edits because your thoughts weren't fully there. That's not a lack of discipline—that's just how the brain works.

So the real problem with multitasking isn't that you're "busy." It's that you're **burning energy on switching**, and that leads to mental fatigue and messy output.

The illusion of productivity in multitasking comes from the false sense of accomplishment we feel when checking off multiple items. But true productivity isn't about quantity—it's about quality and efficiency. Studies show that single-tasking can improve performance by up to 40% compared to multitasking. When we focus on one task at a time, we enter a state of flow, where our attention is undivided, and our work becomes effortless.

So why do we still cling to multitasking? Part of it is societal pressure—being "busy" is often equated with being important." But another reason is habit. Even when the evidence says otherwise, we've trained ourselves to think that doing more at once is better. Breaking this habit requires intentional effort, but the rewards—greater focus, reduced stress, and higher-quality output—are well worth it.

**Identify three tasks you often multitask with.**

- Track how often you switch between tasks in an hour.
- Note any errors or inefficiencies caused by divided attention.

## The Science Behind Single-Tasking

Single-tasking isn't just some cute productivity trick—it's how your brain works best.

When you focus on one thing, your brain can actually go deep. You're using the part that handles planning, decision-making, and real attention. That's why you solve problems faster, think more clearly, and come up with better ideas. But when you multitask, your brain shifts into "quick reaction mode." You might feel busy, but the work stays shallow—like you're skimming the surface instead of diving in.

And here's the big reason: **switching costs**. Every time you jump from one task to another—email to spreadsheet to WhatsApp to meeting notes—your brain has to reset and reorient. That reset takes energy and time. Even small interruptions add up, and by the end of the day you feel tired without really feeling accomplished.

Single-tasking also helps with memory. When you're fully present, your brain stores information better. That's why students who study without distractions usually remember more—and why meetings are more useful when you're not half-checking your phone.

So how do you actually practice single-tasking in a world full of distractions?

### Simple ways to build the habit

*Use focused time blocks. Even 25 minutes of deep focus (Pomodoro style) is powerful.*

*Turn off notifications. If it's not urgent, it can wait.*

*Batch small tasks. Emails, calls, and admin—group them instead of doing them all day.*

*Create a "focus zone." A desk, a corner, headphones—anything that tells your brain: this is work time."*

Train your attention gently. A few minutes of mindfulness a day helps you notice when your mind wanders and bring it back.

One more thing: people often avoid single-tasking because of FOMO—like "if I don't stay available, I'll miss something." But being available all the time usually means you finish less, feel more stressed, and carry half-done work everywhere.

Start small. Pick **one high-impact task** each day and give it **uninterrupted attention**. No switching. No scrolling. Just one thing. You'll be surprised how quickly the work moves—and how much calmer you feel.

```
Single-tasking isn't just about getting more done. It's
about getting your mind back.
```

# 17

# The 80/20 Rule in Time Management.

## The Power of the Pareto Principle

The **80/20 Rule** (also called the Pareto Principle) is one of those ideas that can completely change how you use your time—because it forces you to face an uncomfortable truth:

The majority of your daily activities don't truly make a significant impact.

The basic idea is simple: **80% of your results come from 20% of your effort.** It was first noticed by an economist named Vilfredo Pareto when he saw that a small percentage of people held most of the wealth. But the same pattern shows up everywhere—work, habits, relationships, business, even health.

Now think about your own day. A small number of things you do—maybe one key meeting, a client proposal, deep work on a project, or a tough conversation you've been avoiding—creates most of your progress. But the rest of your day often disappears into low-impact stuff: emails, tiny admin tasks, meetings that could've been messages, and distractions that feel "urgent" but don't really matter.

That's where the 80/20 rule becomes powerful. It's not about working harder. It's about asking:

**"What's the small set of actions that gives me the biggest results?"**

Take Sarah, a marketing executive who felt constantly overwhelmed. She tracked her week and realized something surprising: only a few tasks—like client proposals and leading her team—actually drove results. The rest was noise: endless emails, reports no one read, and small tasks that ate hours. Once she delegated and cut down the low-impact work, she got time back and started performing better *without* burning out.

And once you start looking through the 80/20 lens, you see it everywhere:

- a few clients bring most of the revenue
- a few habits create most of your health and energy
- a few skills make you far more valuable at work

The challenge isn't understanding the rule—it's identifying *your* 20%. That takes reflection, a bit of tracking, and the courage to stop giving your best time to things that don't really matter—even if they feel urgent.

## Identifying Your High-Impact Activities

If you really want to use the 80/20 Rule in real life, the first step is simple—but most people skip it: **you have to get honest about where your time is actually going.**

Because most of us *think* we know. But when you actually track it, it's usually... surprising.

### Step 1: Do a simple time audit (no drama, just truth)

For one week, write down what you do—nothing fancy. Just quick notes like:

- "Checked email – 12 min"
- "Client call – 45 min"
- "Scrolling – 20 min"
- "Writing – 60 min"
- "Meeting – 1 hour"

At the end of the week, look at the list and sort your tasks into three buckets:

1. **High-impact (moves your goals forward)**
2. Examples: writing your book, closing deals, exercising, building relationships, deep work.
3. **Looks productive, but doesn't really matter much**
4. Examples: organizing files, tweaking small details, attending meetings that don't need you.
5. **Straight-up distractions**
6. Examples: mindless scrolling, random multitasking, jumping between apps.

Now ask yourself:

- **What actually created results this week?**
- **What ate time but gave little back?**

You'll usually find the pattern fast: a small set of tasks is doing most of the heavy lifting.

## Step 2: Prioritize like you mean it

Once you know your "top 20%," the next step is being ruthless—in a calm way.

If something doesn't align with your big goals, you have three options:

- **Delegate it** (someone else can handle it)
- **Automate it** (templates, tools, systems)
- **Reduce or remove it** (say no, simplify, stop doing it)

This doesn't mean you ignore boring responsibilities. It just means you stop letting them take over your best hours.

The Eisenhower Matrix helps here: it separates what's urgent from what's actually important. Because many tasks feel urgent, but don't deserve your prime energy.

As Stephen Covey said:

**"The key is not to prioritize what's on your schedule, but to schedule your priorities."**

## Step 3: Protect your high-impact time like it's sacred

If your 20% is writing, then writing needs a real spot on your calendar.

If your 20% is building relationships, schedule those calls.

If your 20% is learning a skill, block time for it weekly.

Because if you don't protect it, the "busy stuff" will always win.

A good rule: **give your best energy to your best tasks.**

Not leftover energy. Not "if I get time." Real time.

# 18

# The Role of Energy, Not Just Time.

"Time is a created thing. To say 'I don't have time' is like saying, 'I don't want to.'"- Lao Tzu

We've all been told that time management is the holy grail of getting things done. We buy the planners, color-code the calendars, and stack our to-do lists like a game of Tetris.

But here's the reality: you can have the most "perfect" schedule in the world and still feel like you're spinning your wheels. Why? This is because a calendar is indifferent to your state of exhaustion.

**The Hidden Engine of Productivity**

Time is finite—we all get the same 24 hours. But **energy** is a different story. Your mental, emotional, and physical "battery" is the real currency of your day. If you try to tackle a complex, high-focus project when your brain is in a 3:00 PM fog, it's going to take you twice as long and feel twice as hard.

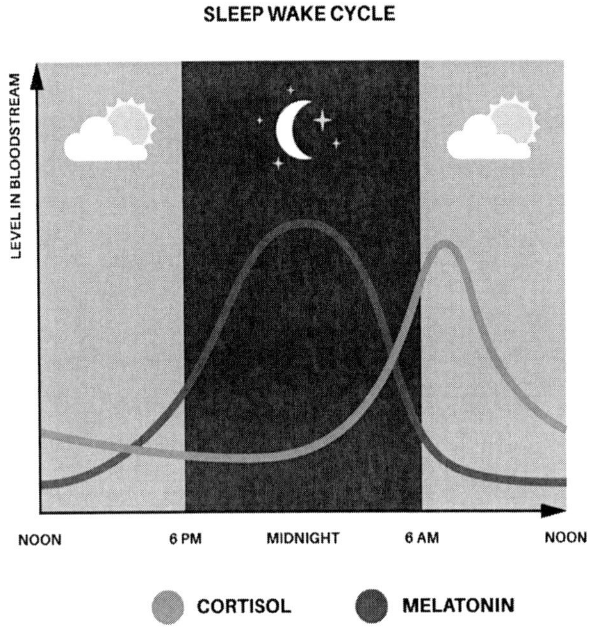


### Work With Your Body, Not Against It

In this chapter, we're shifting the focus. Instead of just managing minutes, we're going to look at managing your **rhythms**. By learning how to align your hardest tasks with your natural peaks of energy, you can:

- **Stop the "Grind":** Achieve more while actually doing less.
- **Kill the Burnout:** Protect your mental health by knowing when to push and when to pivot.
- **Find Your Flow:** Make productivity feel like a natural state rather than a constant uphill battle.

## The Science of Energy Peaks and Valleys

We've been conditioned to think of productivity as a marathon—a grueling, eight-hour race against the clock. But humans aren't machines; we don't have a constant power supply. We have a battery that drains and recharges in waves. If you want to achieve more without burning out, you have to stop managing your minutes and start managing your **rhythms**.

### Stop Fighting Your Biology

Your body runs on a biological clock called the **circadian rhythm**. It dictates when you're a genius and when you're a zombie. Most people follow a standard curve: a morning peak, a post-lunch slump, and a smaller second wind in the late afternoon.

However, your "chronotype" matters. If you're a **morning lark,** tackling deep work at 8:00 AM feels effortless. If you're a **night owl,** forcing that same task before noon is a recipe for brain fog. The key is to map your energy landscape. Track your focus for a week and identify your "peak windows." Allocate your high-stakes, creative work to those times, and reserve the routine emails for periods of lower energy.

### The 8-Hour Myth

The traditional 9-to-5 is a relic of the industrial age. Research shows that the most productive people don't work in marathons; they work in **sprints**—roughly 52 minutes of intense focus followed by a 17-minute break. Your brain thrives on these cycles of work and recovery. When you push through fatigue, you hit "ego depletion," where your willpower and decision-making abilities simply evaporate.

To fuel these sprints, focus on the basics:

- **Movement:** A 5-minute walk can boost creativity by 60%.
- **Fuel:** Think of food as brain fuel; avoid sugar crashes and stay hydrated.
- **Sleep:** 7-9 hours isn't a luxury; it's a performance requirement.

### Deadlines: The GPS of Action

If energy is the fuel, deadlines are the GPS. Without them, we drift. But for many, "deadline" is synonymous with "anxiety." To correct this, we need to understand the **Zeigarnik Effect**: our brains hate unfinished business. An open task generates mental tension that only a completed task can alleviate.

To set deadlines that actually work:

1. **Double It:** We're victims of the "planning fallacy"—we chronically underestimate how long things take. Estimate the time needed, then double it.
2. **Micro-Deadlines:** Break a three-month project into weekly "mini-wins" to maintain momentum.
3. **Accountability:** Tell someone your due date. Social pressure is a powerful motivator.

### Stress is a tool.

Stress isn't inherently bad. The **Yerkes-Dodson Law** shows that performance actually peaks under moderate pressure. This condition is "eustress"—the healthy tension that keeps you sharp. The trick is to keep it manageable. If you're stuck, use the **5-Second Rule**: count down 5-4-3-2-1 and just start. Momentum is the greatest cure for procrastination.

At the end of the day, mastering your time isn't about racing the clock. It's about aligning your effort with your energy and using deadlines as bridges between your intentions and your results.

Below is a template you can use to track your energy for the next five days.

### *The 5-Day Energy Audit*

For the next week, set an alarm for every two hours. When it goes off, rate your **Focus** and **Energy** on a scale of 1–10.

**What to look for:**

- **The Peak:** Your "Golden Window." This is when you should do your hardest, most important work.
- **The Trough:** Your "Slump." This is when you should do "low-brain" tasks (admin, filing, deleting emails).
- **The Rebound:** Your "Second Wind." This is usually a great time for collaborative work or meetings.

**Your Personalized Weekly Tracker**

**Time**

**Energy (1-10)**

**Focus (1-10)**

**What was I doing?**

8:00 AM

10:00 AM

12:00 PM

2:00 PM

4:00 PM

6:00 PM

**How to use these results:**

Once you see the pattern, you can apply **task-energy alignment.** For example, if you find your energy peaks at 10:00 AM but you're spending that time in a status meeting, you're wasting your most valuable biological resource on a low-value task.

Once you've filled out that energy audit for a few days, you'll likely see a pattern emerge. Most people fall into one of three "rhythms." Take a look at these profiles to see which one feels like you:

### *1. The Early Bird (The Morning Lark)*

- **Peak:** 7:00 AM – 11:00 AM.
- **The Move:** Do your hardest "Deep Work" before lunch.
- **The Trap:** Spending your morning answering emails or in stand-up meetings. That's like using high-octane fuel for a lawnmower.

### *2. The Mid-Day Cruiser (The Third Bird)*

- **Peak:** 10:00 AM – 2:00 PM.
- **The Move:** Use the early morning for "warm-up" tasks, then hit your big projects right as the coffee kicks in.
- **The Trap:** Letting the lunch slump (usually 2:00 PM – 4:00 PM) trick you into thinking you're "lazy." It's just your body's natural dip.

### *3. The Night Owl (The Owl)*

- **Peak:** 6:00 PM – 10:00 PM (or later).
- **The Move:** Protect your evenings for your most creative or difficult work. Use the traditional 9-to-5 hours for meetings and administrative tasks.
- **The Trap:** Forcing yourself to be "on" at 8:00 AM. You're fighting

a losing battle against your DNA.

### *Let's build your "Ideal Day"*

Once you have your data, try this **Redesign Exercise**:

1. **Identify your "Deep Work Block":** This is a non-negotiable 90-minute window during your **Peak**. Block it out on your calendar as "Busy."
2. **Identify your "Admin Zone":** This is a 60-minute window during your **Trough** (slump). This is for emails, filing, and mindless tasks.
3. **Identify your "Recovery Window":** A 20-minute gap right after your peak. Go for a walk, grab water, or just stare at a wall. **Do not look at a screen.**

Let's use a "**Knowledge Worker**" template. This works for students, writers, developers, or anyone who has to use their brain to solve problems.

Here's how we can organize your life into a schedule that truly brings you joy:

### *Step 1: Slot the "Big Rocks" (High Energy)*

These are tasks that require **Deep Work**—problem-solving, writing, or strategic thinking.

- **When:** Your Peak (e.g., 9:00 AM – 11:00 AM).
- **The Rule:** No phone, no "quick" email checks, and no Slack. These tasks are the most mentally expensive; pay for them when your

"account" is full.

### *Step 2: Slot the "Shallow Work" (Low Energy)*

These are tasks that are necessary but don't require much brainpower—expense reports, booking travel, or clearing out your inbox.

- **When:** Your Trough (e.g., 2:00 PM – 3:30 PM).
- **The Strategy:** Batch these. Don't do them one by one throughout the day. Save them for when you're feeling a bit sluggish.

### *Step 3: Slot the "Interpersonal Work" (Mixed Energy)*

Meetings, phone calls, and brainstorming.

- **When:** Your Rebound (e.g., 4:00 PM – 5:00 PM).
- **Why:** Talking to others often provides an external energy boost that helps carry you through the end of the day.

### *The "Ideal Day" Blueprint*

Here is what the final "redesign" looks like on a calendar:

**Zone**- **08:00 - 09:00**
**Activity Type**-Ramp Up
**Example Task**- Review goals, light reading, coffee.

**09:00 - 11:30**
**DEEP WORK**
Complex coding, writing a proposal.
**11:30 - 12:30**
Break / Fuel

Healthy lunch, 15-minute walk.

**12:30 - 14:00**

Collaborative

Team meetings or 1:1s.

**14:00 - 15:30**

**ADMIN SLUMP**

Emails, filing, data entry.

**15:30 - 17:00**

Second Wind

This time is dedicated to creative brainstorming and planning for tomorrow.

```
One final trick: The "Shutdown Ritual"
At the end of your workday, take 5 minutes to write down the
one big thing you need to do during your Peak tomorrow. This
prevents "Zeigarnik stress"--that nagging feeling that
you've forgotten something--and lets your brain actually
rest at night.
```

# 19

# The Joy of Time Blocking

"Time is not a resource to be spent, but a canvas to be painted. Master the brush, and you master your life."

Time blocking isn't just a fancy productivity trick—it's a way of taking your day back.

Instead of living off an endless to-do list (where tasks just pile up and everything feels urgent), time blocking puts your priorities on the calendar. It turns your day into a plan you can actually follow. You stop reacting to whatever pops up next and start deciding—deliberately—what gets your time and attention.

Think of it like this: a to-do list tells you *what* you should do. Time blocking tells you *when* you'll do it. And that "when" is what makes things real.

In this chapter, we'll break down how time blocking works, why it's so effective, and how to use it in a realistic way—whether you're a CEO stuck in meetings all day, a student trying to balance classes and projects, or just someone who wants to stop ending the day thinking, "Where did all my time go?"

## The Science Behind Time Blocking

Your brain is built to focus on one thing at a time—not to bounce between emails, calls, messages, and five half-finished tasks. And every time you switch, there's a cost. It might feel like you're "staying on top of things," but mentally you're just reopening the same file again and again. That's why task-switching can kill productivity and leave you exhausted without much to show for it.

Time blocking fixes that by giving your brain what it actually needs: **clear, uninterrupted chunks of time for one job.** When you're not constantly switching lanes, you hit that "locked in" mode—where work feels smoother and you get more done in less time. Multitasking is like driving through traffic with nonstop lane changes. Time blocking is the express lane.

It also takes advantage of something simple but real: **work expands to fill the time you give it.** If you tell yourself a report will take three hours, it'll somehow take three hours. But if you block 90 minutes, you're more likely to focus, cut the fluff, and get it done faster. Deadlines create clarity.

And time blocking isn't only about efficiency—it's about saving mental energy. Every day you waste a surprising amount of brainpower deciding what to do next. When your day is already planned, you stop negotiating with yourself every hour. You just follow the plan, and that reduces decision fatigue so you have more energy for the work that actually matters.

Finally, it works best when it matches your natural rhythm. Most people think better in the morning, so that's a great time for deep work—writing, strategy, studying, problem-solving. Afternoons often work better for lighter tasks like emails, admin, follow-ups. When your blocks match your energy, the whole day feels less like a fight.

## How to Design Your Ideal Time Block System

### *Step 1: Audit Your Current Schedule*

Before building a new system, diagnose the old one. Track your time for a week using apps like Toggl or a simple spreadsheet. Note:

- How much time is spent on productive vs. reactive tasks (e.g., emails, social media)
- When you're most focused vs. fatigued
- Recurring time-wasters (e.g., unnecessary meetings)

### *Step 2: Categorize Your Tasks*

Divide tasks into:

- Deep Work Blocks (60–90 mins): High-focus tasks like writing, coding, or strategizing.
- Shallow Work Blocks (30 mins): Administrative tasks like emails or invoicing.
- Flex Blocks (15–30 mins): Buffer time for unexpected demands.

### *Step 3: Assign Time Blocks*

Use a digital calendar (Google Calendar, Outlook) or a paper planner. Color-code categories for visual clarity. For example:

- Blue for deep work
- Green for meetings
- Yellow for personal time

### *Step 4: Protect Your Blocks*

Treat time blocks like unbreakable appointments. If a colleague requests a meeting during a deep work block, politely decline or suggest an alternative slot.

### *Step 5: Review and Adapt*

At week's end, assess:

- Which blocks were consistently interrupted?
- Did certain tasks need more/less time?
- Were energy levels aligned with task difficulty?

## Common Time Blocking Mistakes (And How to Fix Them)

**Mistake 1: Overstuffing Blocks**

Packing too many tasks into a block leads to rush and stress. *Fix:* Follow the "50/70 Rule"—fill only 50–70% of your day with structured tasks, leaving room for spontaneity.

**Mistake 2: Ignoring Transition Time**

Switching from a client call to a creative sprint without a break drains focus. *Fix:* Insert 5–10 minute "breathing blocks" between major tasks to reset.

**Mistake 3: Rigid Scheduling**

Life is unpredictable. A sick child or a server crash can derail your plan. *Fix:* Include "flex blocks" to absorb disruptions without collapsing your entire schedule.

**Mistake 4: Neglecting Personal Time**

Productivity isn't just about work. *Fix:* Block time for exercise, family, and hobbies. As author Cal Newport states, "A schedule defends against *chaos and whim.*"

**Mistake 5: Abandoning the System Too Soon**

New habits take 21+ days to stick. *Fix:* Commit to time blocking for a month before judging its efficacy.

## Advanced Time Blocking Techniques

**Theme Days**

Popularized by Elon Musk and Jack Dorsey, this method dedicates entire days to specific themes (e.g., Mondays for meetings, Tuesdays for product development). It reduces context-switching and deepens expertise in focused areas.

**The Pomodoro-Plus Method**

Combine time blocking with Pomodoro (25-minute sprints + 5-minute breaks), but adjust durations to match task complexity. For deep work, try 90-minute blocks with 20-minute breaks.

**Task Batching**

Group similar shallow tasks (e.g., replying to emails, making calls) into a single block to minimize mental gear-shifting.

**Reverse Time Blocking**

Start by blocking personal commitments (sleep, meals, family time), then fit work around them. This ensures life doesn't become an afterthought.

## The Psychological Benefits of Time Blocking

Beyond productivity, time blocking nurtures mental well-being. A *Harvard Business Review* study found that employees with clear boundaries between work and personal time reported 30% higher job satisfaction. Here's why:

1. Reduced Anxiety: A plan eliminates the "What should I do next?" panic.
2. Enhanced Presence: When you're in a "family block," you're fully engaged—not distracted by work guilt.
3. Achievement Momentum: Checking off completed blocks releases dopamine, reinforcing productive habits.
4. Control Restoration: In a world of endless demands, time blocking is your declaration of autonomy.

```
"The key is not to prioritize what's on your schedule, but
to schedule your priorities." --Stephen Covey
```

By mastering time blocking, you're not just organizing your day—you're architecting a life of intention, balance, and joy.

# 20

# The Power of Reflection.

"We do not learn from experience... we learn from reflecting on experience."
- John Dewey

**Reflection: The Key to Controlling Your Time**

Imagine that you are at the end of a long day and gazing at your calendar. You have successfully completed tasks, sent emails, and navigated through meetings. But did it matter? Did it bring you closer to the life you want? Planning and working hard can feel heroic, but the real magic—the spark that turns effort into unstoppable momentum—is looking back.

It's that calm moment when you think, "What worked?" What didn't work? What is one modification that makes a big difference? Reflection is not busywork. It's the difference between going in circles and flying toward your goals. This chapter will show you how to turn time into success through reflection, whether you're a student studying for tests, a sales manager achieving targets, or a parent trying to do it all.

## Why Reflection Is Your Best Friend

We've all been there, running from one thing to the next on autopilot, wondering why we're so tired but not ahead. Thinking about things stops the chaos. It's like having a coach that watches your game footage and tells you how to win next time.

For example, take Raj, a 28-year-old pharmaceutical sales representative from Jharkhand . He was overwhelmed with goals, late nights, and no time for his personal life. Then he spent ten minutes at night thinking about his day and writing down his wins, energy drains, and things that bothered him. He knew that calls from clients after 5 PM made it difficult for him to pay attention. He moved them to the mornings and stopped creative planning in the afternoons. His sales went up by 35% in just a few weeks, and he had time in the evenings for his YouTube channel. Reflection didn't add hours; it amplified them.

Science supports it: Studies of behavior reveal that those who think about things improve 20–30% faster. Why? Thinking about things triggers a feedback cycle. You celebrate wins (which release dopamine), find leaks (which are like email black holes), and change direction quickly. All of a sudden, you're not just busy; you're getting things done.

## Life-Changing Stories of Self-Awareness

Reflection isn't just cold analysis; it's a mirror that shows you who you really are. It shows you what makes you feel things, what habits you don't know you have, and what your real energy patterns are.

Neuroscientists claim it changes the way your prefrontal cortex works so you can make better judgments and regulate your impulses. It's like upgrading your brain's operating system.

Priya is a college student who has a lot of work to do. One negative grade report showed her that social media took up two hours of her day after "quick checks." Every night, she thought about how she felt. She felt frustrated and scattered. She scrolled in groups for 20 minutes after studying. Her stress levels have decreased, her grades have improved, and her confidence has skyrocketed. She didn't gain time; she got it back.

Or think about Vikram, a CEO who hated having meetings with his workforce. Reflection revealed that his worry made him speak incoherently. He noticed how people were reacting (heart beating), thought about what to do (team disengaged), and made a strategy (stop, breathe, and listen first). Meetings turned into big steps forward. Being self-aware isn't a waste of time; it's your superpower.

**Experience transforms into battle-tested wisdom.**

Imagine two individuals participating in a marathon. One person keeps track of their mileage without thinking about it, while the other breaks down every run into pace, fuel, and recovery. Who do you think will cross the finish line first? Life is the same as reflection. It turns missteps into steps.

Arun, the startup founder, was on the verge of burning out. Arun made too many promises each week, which perpetuated the cycle of overcommitment. Arun's fear of saying no became evident through reflection. He began counting "no's" as wins. He successfully streamlined projects and doubled revenue. We can't see patterns like procrastination loops or priority mismatches without thinking about them. With it? Wisdom builds on itself, like interest.

And what about being thankful? It's the fuel for the rocket. Research from UC Berkeley demonstrates that it helps people stay strong in the face of chaos. At the end of the day, write down three wins: a challenging call you made and a habit you kept to. Do you feel that lift? It's reflection that keeps your fire going.

Five minutes tonight is your first step. What made you feel positive? What made you tired? Consider making a change tomorrow. Watch how the momentum grows.

# 21

# The Art of Delegation.

```
"You can do anything, but not everything." - David Allen
```

Delegation isn't just a "manager thing." It's a survival skill—especially when your days are already packed and your brain is running on fumes.

A lot of us resist delegating for completely human reasons. We often think, "It will be more efficient if I handle it personally," or "They will not execute it according to my standards," or "Delegating this task will cause me to lose oversight." And sometimes, yes—delegating takes some effort upfront. But once it's set up, it provides you something back that you can't buy: **time and mental space.**

Here's the truth: **every minute you spend doing work that someone else could do is a minute you're stealing from your highest-value work.** The things only you can do—strategy, decision-making, creativity, relationship-building, and leading—deserve your best energy. This does not apply to administrative tasks, follow-ups, formatting, scheduling, or repetitive busywork.

Rashmi, a startup founder, learned this the hard way. In her first year she tried to do everything—client calls, operations, social media, even tiny tasks that didn't really need her. She believed no one would meet her standards, so she carried it all. The result? burnout was right around the corner. When she finally started trusting her team and delegating the smaller stuff, her whole business improved. She had more time for growth decisions, and she actually got her life back.

Delegation isn't dumping work on people. It's choosing where your energy should go—and building support for everything else.

The reluctance to delegate often stems from perfectionism or fear of losing authority. But research in organizational psychology reveals that teams thrive when leaders empower them with responsibility. Delegation fosters trust, builds competence, and creates a collaborative environment where everyone grows. The first step is recognizing that holding onto every task is a form of self-sabotage. To master your time management, you must learn to let go of certain tasks.

## Identifying What to Delegate

Not every task should be delegated, but many can—and should—be. The key is distinguishing between high-value tasks (those that align with your core strengths and goals) and low-value tasks (those that drain your time without significant return). A simple framework to determine what to delegate is the **Eisenhower Matrix**, which categorizes tasks into four quadrants: urgent and important, important but not urgent, urgent but not important, and neither urgent nor important. Tasks in the last two categories are prime candidates for delegation.

For example, administrative work like scheduling meetings, data entry, or routine emails often falls into the "urgent but not important" category. These tasks consume time without contributing meaningfully to your long-term objectives. By delegating them, you free up mental bandwidth for strategic thinking, creative problem-solving, or relationship-building—activities that truly move the needle in your personal and professional life.

Another useful filter is the **"Only I Can Do This" test**. Ask yourself: *Is this something only I am qualified or authorized to handle?* If the answer is no, it's likely delegable. Even tasks that require some oversight can be partially delegated. For instance, if you're writing a report, you might draft the research outline but assign data collection to a team member.

**Tasks that are repetitive and time-consuming**

- Tasks outside your core expertise
- Tasks that others can perform just as well (or better)
- Tasks that provide growth opportunities for team members
- Tasks that don't require your direct decision-making

## Choosing the Right People

Delegation fails when the wrong person is assigned a task. The key is matching the task to someone's skills, interests, and developmental needs. Start by assessing your team's (or network's) strengths. Who excels at detail-oriented work? Who thrives in creative problem-solving? Who is eager to take on more responsibility? Effective delegation isn't just about offloading work—it's about empowering others to succeed.

Take the example of Raj, a project manager who struggled with delegation until he started aligning tasks with his team's passions. He noticed one team member loved visual storytelling, so he delegated presentation design to her. Another had a knack for analytics, so he handed over data reporting. Not only did the quality of work improve, but his team also became more engaged and motivated.

Trust is critical. If you delegate but micromanage, you defeat the purpose. Instead, provide clear expectations and autonomy. Use the **"5 Levels of Delegation"** framework by management expert Jurgen Appelo:

1. Tell – You decide and instruct.
2. Sell – You explain why the task matters.
3. Consult – You ask for input before deciding.
4. Agree – You collaborate on the decision.
5. Delegate – You hand over full responsibility.

The higher the level, the more ownership the delegatee feels. Start with lower levels for new tasks or inexperienced team members, then gradually increase autonomy as trust builds.

## Communicating Clearly

One of the biggest pitfalls in delegation is unclear instructions. Vague requests like "Handle this project" set everyone up for frustration. Instead, use the **SMART criteria** to frame delegated tasks:

- Specific – What exactly needs to be done?
- Measurable – How will success be evaluated?
- Achievable – Is the task realistic given resources?
- Relevant – How does it align with broader goals?
- Time-bound – What's the deadline?

For example, instead of saying, "Can you work on the client proposal?" say, "Draft a 10-page proposal for Client X, focusing on our sustainability solutions, by Friday at 3 PM. Include three case studies and budget breakdown." The clearer the instructions, the higher the chance of success.

Regular check-ins are also crucial. Schedule brief updates to monitor progress without hovering. Use questions like:

- "What's working well so far?"
- "Are there any roadblocks?"
- "Do you need additional resources?"

This keeps communication open while respecting the delegatee's autonomy.

## Overcoming Delegation Guilt

Many people feel guilty about delegating, as if they're burdening others. But reframe it: delegation is an opportunity for growth—for you *and* the person taking on the task. When you delegate, you're not just freeing your time; you're helping others develop new skills, gain confidence, and contribute meaningfully.

If guilt persists, consider this: by hoarding tasks, you're denying others the chance to step up. Leadership isn't about doing it all—it's about enabling others to shine. Start small. Please consider delegating a minor task this week and take some time to reflect on the outcomes. You'll likely find that the world doesn't collapse—in fact, things might run smoother.

> "The best leaders don't create followers. They create more leaders." - Tom Peters

Delegation is a muscle that strengthens with practice. The more you do it, the more natural it becomes. And as you master this art, you'll find yourself with more time, less stress, and a team (or support system) that's more capable and motivated than ever. Your minutes—and your life—will thank you.

# 22

# The Science of Goal Setting.

"A goal properly set is halfway reached." — Zig Ziglar

Goals are the compass that guides our daily actions, turning abstract dreams into tangible achievements. But not all goals are created equal. The difference between success and stagnation often lies in how we frame our objectives. In this chapter, we'll explore the science behind effective goal setting, how to align them with your time management strategy, and the psychological principles that make them stick.

## Why Goals Matter in Time Management

Without clear goals, time management is like sailing without a destination—you might move fast, but you won't necessarily arrive where you want to be. Goals provide structure, motivation, and a measurable way to track progress. Research from Harvard Business School shows that people who set specific goals are **10 times more likely to succeed** than those who don't. But why?

First, goals activate the **Reticular Activating System (RAS)** in our brain, a neural network that filters information and highlights opportunities related to our objectives. When you set a goal—say, "I want to write a book"—your brain starts noticing writing tips, publishing advice, and time management strategies that align with that ambition. Second, goals create **accountability**. When you write down a goal, you're more likely to commit to it, thanks to the psychological principle of **consistency bias**—our innate desire to align our actions with our stated intentions.

However, vague goals like "I want to be successful" or "I need to be more productive" don't work because they lack clarity. Instead, we need **SMART goals**—Specific, Measurable, Achievable, Relevant, and Time-bound. For example, "I will write 500 words every morning for the next 30 days" is a SMART goal because it defines what, how much, and by when.

To integrate goals into your time management system, follow these steps:

Identify your long-term vision (e.g., career growth, personal development)

1. Break it into smaller, actionable steps
2. Assign deadlines to each step
3. Schedule them into your calendar and Review progress weekly

By doing this, you transform abstract aspirations into **time-bound commitments**, ensuring that every minute you spend moves you closer to success.

## The Psychology of Effective Goal Setting

Why do some people achieve their goals while others abandon them within weeks? The answer lies in **behavioral psychology**. Studies show that **90% of New Year's resolutions fail** because people rely on willpower alone, ignoring the science of habit formation.

One key principle is **implementation intentions**, a concept from psychologist Peter Gollwitzer. Instead of saying, "I'll exercise more," you say, "I'll go for a 30-minute run at 7 AM every Monday, Wednesday, and Friday." This specificity **triggers automatic behavior**, reducing decision fatigue. Another critical factor is **loss aversion**—our tendency to fear losing something more than we desire gaining it. If you commit to a goal publicly (e.g., telling friends you're writing a book), the fear of embarrassment can be a powerful motivator.

Additionally, **the Zeigarnik Effect** explains why unfinished tasks stick in our minds. When you start a goal but don't complete it, your brain keeps nagging you—a useful trick to maintain momentum. To leverage this, break goals into **micro-tasks**. For example, instead of "write a book," start with "outline Chapter 1."

Here's how to apply psychology to your goals:

Use "if-then" planning (e.g., "If it's 8 AM, then I'll work on my project")

**Make progress visible (trackers, journals, apps)**
**Reward small wins to reinforce motivation**
**Share goals to create social accountability**
**Reframe setbacks as learning opportunities**

By understanding these mental triggers, you can design goals that **stick** rather than fizzle out.

## The Role of Time Blocking in Goal Achievement

Goals without a time plan are just wishes. That's where **time blocking** comes in—a method where you assign specific time slots to tasks, turning goals into scheduled actions. Elon Musk, Bill Gates, and Cal Newport swear by this technique because it prevents **task diffusion** (scattered, unproductive work).

For example, if your goal is to learn a new language, you might block 30 minutes daily for Duolingo practice. This ensures consistency, which is crucial for mastery. Research from the University of London found that people who time-block are **40% more productive** because it reduces multitasking and context-switching.

To implement time blocking effectively:

### Prioritize High-Impact Goals – Focus on tasks that align with your long-term vision.

Batch Similar Tasks – Group related activities (e.g., emails, calls) to minimize mental switching costs.

Buffer Time – Leave gaps for unexpected interruptions.

Review & Adjust – At week's end, assess what worked and refine your schedule.

"You will never find time for anything. You must make it." — Charles Buxton

By treating time blocking as a non-negotiable appointment with your goals, you ensure steady progress.

## Overcoming Common Goal-Setting Pitfalls

Even with the best intentions, people often fall into traps that derail their goals. Let's examine the most common mistakes and how to avoid them:

### 1. Setting Too Many Goals

Ambition is great, but spreading yourself too thin leads to burnout. **Research from Stanford shows that** multitasking reduces productivity by up to 40%. **Instead, focus on** 1-3 key goals** at a time.

## 2. Ignoring Energy Levels

Your willpower fluctuates throughout the day. Schedule demanding tasks during peak energy (e.g., morning for most people) and save low-energy tasks (like admin work) for later.

## 3. Lack of Flexibility

Rigid goals break under pressure. Build **contingency time** for setbacks. If you miss a workout, adjust—don't abandon the goal entirely.

## 4. No Measurement System

If you don't track progress, you can't improve. Use apps, journals, or spreadsheets to monitor milestones.

## 5. Fear of Failure

Perfectionism kills progress. Embrace "**good enough**" and iterate. Thomas Edison didn't fail 1,000 times—he found 1,000 ways that didn't work.

By anticipating these pitfalls, you can design **resilient goals** that withstand real-world challenges.

## Case Study: How SMART Goals Transformed a CEO's Productivity

To illustrate these principles, let's look at Rehana, a startup CEO who struggled with time management. She worked 12-hour days but felt unproductive. After adopting SMART goals and time blocking, she:

*Clarified her top 3 quarterly objectives (e.g., increase revenue by 20%)*

*Broke them into weekly targets (e.g., "Close 5 new clients")*

*Assigned time blocks (e.g., "Sales calls: Tuesdays 10 AM–12 PM")*

*Tracked progress in a dashboard*

Within six months, her revenue grew by **25%**, and she reclaimed 10+ hours weekly for family. Her secret? **Goals weren't just ideas—they were scheduled actions.**

## Final Thoughts: Your Goal-Setting Blueprint

Mastering the science of goal setting transforms how you use time. To recap:

Use **SMART criteria** to define clear objectives

- Leverage **psychology** (implementation intentions, loss aversion)
- **Time-block** goals into your schedule
- **Avoid common pitfalls** (overcommitment, rigidity)
- **Measure and adapt** for continuous improvement

```
Now, take your biggest goal and apply these steps today.
Remember, time doesn't wait-but you can command it.
```

# 23

# The Role of Mindfulness in Productivity.

```
"Mindfulness is the secret ingredient to peak performance.
It's not about doing more; it's about being fully present in
what you do." - Dr. Ellen Langer, Harvard Psychologist
```

## The Science of Mindfulness and Focus

Mindfulness isn't just a trendy word; it's a practical, science-backed way to get more done with less stress. Researchers at places like Harvard and Stanford have found that regular mindfulness practice can actually change the brain, helping people focus better, feel calmer, and remember more. When you're mindful, the prefrontal cortex—the part of your brain that handles focus and decision-making—steps up, while the amygdala, which drives stress and fight-or-flight reactions, quiets down. This shift helps you approach your work with clarity instead of anxiety or impulse.

Think of a busy executive handling back-to-back meetings, emails, and decisions. Without mindfulness, it's simple to operate automatically, make hasty decisions, and overlook crucial details. With mindfulness, that same person learns to pause, breathe, and consciously choose what matters most in the moment.

Neuroscientist Dr. Amishi Jha has shown through her research with soldiers under intense stress that even around 12 minutes of mindfulness practice a day can noticeably improve focus and mental stability under pressure. The same idea applies to students, professionals, creators, and entrepreneurs: mindfulness isn't about slowing your life down—it's about sharpening your mind so you can work smarter, not just harder.

One common misconception is that mindfulness requires hours of meditation. In reality, even micro-practices—like taking three deep breaths before a meeting or savoring a sip of coffee—can reset your focus. The key is consistency. Just as physical exercise builds muscle over time, mindfulness strengthens your mental resilience.

- Start with 5 minutes of mindful breathing each morning
- Practice single-tasking instead of multitasking for one hour daily
- Notice when your mind wanders and gently bring it back to the present
- Use a mindfulness app (e.g., Headspace or Calm) for guided sessions
- Reflect on one thing you're grateful for at the end of each day.

## How Mindfulness Reduces Decision Fatigue

Decision fatigue is the mental exhaustion that comes from making too many choices, leading to poorer decisions as the day progresses. Judges, for example, are more likely to deny parole in the afternoon than in the morning due to depleted mental energy. Mindfulness combats this by creating mental space between stimuli and responses, allowing for more intentional choices.

Steve Jobs, a proponent of mindfulness, famously wore the same outfit daily to eliminate trivial decisions. While not everyone needs a uniform, simplifying routines—like meal prepping or scheduling "deep work" blocks—can conserve cognitive bandwidth. Mindfulness also helps us recognize when we're operating on autopilot, such as scrolling social media instead of working. By bringing awareness to these habits, we can redirect energy toward meaningful tasks.

A study published in *Psychological Science* found that mindfulness practitioners made 20% fewer errors in high-stakes tasks compared to non-practitioners. This is because mindfulness cultivates metacognition—the ability to observe your thinking. Imagine you're about to snap at a colleague during a stressful moment. A mindful pause lets you choose a constructive response instead of reacting impulsively.

To apply this:

1. Batch decisions: Group similar tasks (e.g., answering emails) to minimize context-switching.
2. Set defaults: Automate routines (e.g., workout schedules) to reduce decision load.
3. Pause before reacting: Count to five before responding to a frustrating email.
4. Limit options: When overwhelmed, narrow choices (e.g., "Will this action move me closer to my goal?").

5. Reflect nightly: Review decisions made and note where mindfulness could've helped.

## Mindfulness Techniques for Time Management

Time management isn't just about schedules; it's about attention management. The Pomodoro Technique, for instance, pairs well with mindfulness. Work for 25 minutes, then take a 5-minute mindful break—stretch, breathe, or observe your surroundings. This prevents burnout and keeps focus sharp.

Another technique is "time blocking with intention." Instead of mechanically filling calendars, ask: *What's the purpose of this task?* A CEO might block 30 minutes for "strategic thinking" rather than "meeting prep," framing the time with clarity. Mindfulness also helps combat the planning fallacy—our tendency to underestimate how long tasks take. By staying present, you're more attuned to actual progress versus wishful thinking.

The "STOP" method is a quick mindfulness tool:

**S**top what you're doing
**T**ake a breath
**O**bserve your thoughts and emotions
**P**roceed with intention

For example, a writer struggling with procrastination might STOP, notice their anxiety about the blank page, and then commit to writing just one sentence. Often, momentum follows.

## Mindfulness in High-Stress Environments

Emergency room doctors, soldiers, and air traffic controllers use mindfulness to stay calm under pressure. The same principles apply to deadlines or presentations. Tactical breathing—inhaling for 4 seconds, holding for 4, exhaling for 4—can lower heart rate and sharpen focus.

A study of Fortune 500 leaders found that those who practiced mindfulness reported 30% higher productivity during crises. They could detach from chaos, assess priorities, and delegate effectively. One technique is the "body scan": spend 2 minutes mentally checking in from head to toe, releasing tension. This prevents stress from hijacking productivity.

*"In the midst of movement and chaos, keep stillness inside of you." — Deepak Chopra*

To adapt this for work:

1. Pre-stress ritual: Before a high-pressure event, close your eyes and visualize success.
2. Anchor phrases: Repeat a mantra like "This too shall pass" during overwhelm.
3. Gratitude pauses: Amid chaos, list three things going well to shift perspective.
4. Micro-meditations: Use elevator rides or waits for mindful breathing.
5. Post-stress recovery: After a stressful event, take 5 minutes to reset (e.g., walk or hydrate).

## Cultivating a Mindful Lifestyle for Long-Term Success

Mindfulness isn't a quick fix; it's a lifestyle. Start small—a mindful morning routine sets the tone. Instead of grabbing your phone, spend 5 minutes journaling or sipping tea while observing sunlight. This builds a habit of presence.

Evening reflection is equally vital. Ask:

- What did I accomplish today?
- Where did I lose focus?
- How can I improve tomorrow?

Over time, mindfulness becomes second nature, turning scattered days into purposeful ones. The result? Not just productivity, but a richer, more balanced life.

Create a mindful morning ritual (e.g., no screens for the first 30 minutes)
Use transitions (commutes, lunch breaks) to check in with yourself
End the day with a "mental shutdown" ritual to compartmentalize work stress
Practice active listening in conversations—no multitasking
Schedule quarterly "mindfulness audits" to assess progress

By weaving mindfulness into daily routines, you'll master not just time, but the quality of every minute.

# The Power of Visualization

## How Mental Rehearsals Can Save You Time and Boost Performance

### *The Science Behind Visualization*

Visualization is more than just daydreaming—it's a scientifically validated technique used by elite athletes, CEOs, and high performers to optimize their time and outcomes. Studies in neuroscience reveal that when we vividly imagine performing a task, our brain activates the same neural pathways as when we physically execute it. This mental rehearsal strengthens neural connections, making the actual performance smoother and more efficient. For instance, research on Olympic athletes found that those who combined physical training with mental visualization improved their performance by up to 35% compared to those who relied solely on physical practice. The brain doesn't distinguish between real and imagined actions, which means you can "practice" tasks in your mind, saving valuable time while still reaping the benefits of repetition.

But how does this translate to everyday productivity? Imagine you have a critical presentation coming up. Instead of rehearsing it repeatedly (which could take hours), you could spend 10 minutes visualizing yourself delivering it flawlessly—your tone, gestures, and even handling tough questions with ease. This mental run-through primes your brain to perform confidently, reducing last-minute panic and wasted time on excessive prep. Visualization also helps identify potential obstacles before they arise, allowing you to strategize solutions in advance. For example, if you mentally stumble during a visualized negotiation, you can refine your approach before the real meeting. This proactive problem-solving eliminates time lost to trial and error in real-world scenarios.

Moreover, visualization taps into the Reticular Activating System (RAS), a brain filter that highlights information relevant to your goals. When you consistently visualize success, your RAS starts noticing opportunities and resources that align with your mental imagery. A sales professional visualizing closing deals might suddenly spot a networking event or a key contact they'd previously overlooked. This subconscious guidance streamlines decision-making and prioritization, cutting through distractions and saving hours of unfocused effort. The key is specificity: vague visualizations yield vague results, but detailed mental rehearsals—incorporating sights, sounds, and emotions—create a brain blueprint for success.

*"Visualization is the art of seeing the invisible and believing in the inevitable." — Adapted from Jonathan Swift*

To harness visualization effectively, follow these steps:

Set aside 5–10 minutes daily for focused visualization.

Engage all senses—imagine not just visuals but also sounds, smells, and emotions.

Pair visualization with actionable goals (e.g., "I see myself finishing this report by noon").

Use it to rehearse challenging tasks before executing them.

Reflect on mental rehearsals to identify and correct potential pitfalls.

## Time-Saving Applications of Visualization

Visualization isn't limited to big goals; it's a versatile tool for daily time optimization. Consider mundane tasks like organizing your inbox or meal prepping. By mentally walking through these activities beforehand, you can spot inefficiencies and streamline your approach. For instance, visualizing your ideal morning routine—waking up without hitting snooze, efficiently preparing breakfast, and tackling your top priority—can shave off minutes that add up over weeks. A study at Stanford University found that individuals who visualized their daily schedules completed tasks 20% faster than those who didn't, as mental rehearsal reduced decision fatigue and hesitation.

In professional settings, visualization can compress learning curves. A software developer learning a new programming language might visualize writing code flawlessly, which accelerates mastery by reinforcing neural patterns. Similarly, a project manager could mentally simulate a team meeting, anticipating conflicts and refining their communication strategy. This "failure in the mind" prevents real-world missteps that waste time. Even in high-pressure scenarios, like public speaking, visualization reduces anxiety-induced delays. When your brain has already "experienced" success, you bypass the paralysis of overthinking and act decisively.

Entrepreneurs can leverage visualization for strategic planning. Imagine mentally testing different business pivot scenarios—each visualized outcome reveals potential time sinks or advantages. This foresight helps allocate resources more effectively. For example, a startup founder visualizing customer interactions might realize that a proposed feature isn't as critical as assumed, saving months of development time. Visualization also aids habit formation. By repeatedly imagining yourself exercising at 6 AM or writing 500 words before breakfast, you rewire your brain to make these actions automatic, eliminating the time lost to procrastination.

*"The more vividly you see the path, the fewer detours you'll take."*

Here's how to apply visualization for time savings:

Mentally rehearse repetitive tasks to identify shortcuts.
- Use it to prepare for meetings, reducing unnecessary back-and-forth.
- Visualize overcoming distractions (e.g., ignoring social media alerts).
- Pair it with time-blocking—see yourself adhering to your schedule.
- Reflect weekly on how visualization saved you time.

**Overcoming Common Visualization Pitfalls**

While powerful, visualization can backfire if done incorrectly. One pitfall is passive visualization—vaguely imagining success without emotional engagement. For example, picturing yourself winning a promotion while feeling doubtful reinforces negativity. Instead, attach emotions like confidence and gratitude to your mental imagery. Research from the University of Chicago shows that emotion-laden visualizations are 50% more effective in driving action. Another mistake is over-relying on visualization without action. It's a supplement, not a substitute; visualizing a marathon won't replace training, but it can enhance your regimen.

Perfectionism in visualization also wastes time. Some people obsess over crafting "perfect" mental images, which defeats the purpose of efficiency. The goal is progress, not pixel-perfect detail. Similarly, visualizing unrealistic outcomes (e.g., completing a month's work in a day) sets you up for frustration. Ground your visualizations in achievable steps, like breaking a project into visualized milestones. Lastly, inconsistency dilutes results. Sporadic visualization is like sporadic exercise—ineffective. Commit to daily practice, even for two minutes, to build cumulative benefits.

```
"A flawed plan visualized is better than a perfect plan
imagined."
```

**To avoid these pitfalls:**

Combine visualization with tangible action plans.

- Focus on emotions, not just visuals.
- Keep sessions brief but consistent.
- Align mental rehearsals with realistic goals.
- Adjust visualizations based on real-world feedback.

## Case Studies: Visualization in Action

**Case Study 1: The Athlete's Edge**

Michael, a triathlete, used visualization to cut his training time by 15%. He mentally rehearsed each leg of the race—swimming strokes, transition routines, and pacing—which reduced his actual race-day errors. By visualizing potential hurdles (e.g., fatigue at mile 18), he prepped strategies, saving minutes otherwise lost to hesitation.

**Case Study 2: The Executive's Shortcut**

Priya, a CFO, visualized her quarterly reports process. She imagined consolidating data efficiently and anticipating stakeholder questions. This prep reduced her report completion time from 12 hours to 8, freeing up a workday each quarter.

**Case Study 3: The Student's Hack**

College student Jamal visualized studying without distractions. He mentally "practiced" ignoring his phone and focusing for 45-minute blocks. Within weeks, his study sessions became 30% more productive, reclaiming hours for leisure.

## Integrating Visualization into Your Routine

Start small: dedicate two minutes each morning to visualizing your top priority. Gradually expand to other tasks. Use triggers—like a morning coffee—to anchor the habit. Track your progress in a journal, noting time saved or performance improvements. Over time, this mental tool will become second nature, turning wasted minutes into mastered moments.

***"Time isn't lost; it's just waiting to be visualized."***

Final checklist for integration:

**Begin with one daily visualization session.**

- Use triggers to build consistency.

- Journal outcomes to measure impact.
- Scale up to complex tasks as confidence grows.
- Share techniques with peers to reinforce accountability.

```
By mastering visualization, you're not just saving
time--you're sculpting it.
```

# 24

# The Science of Decision Fatigue.

Decision fatigue is that sneaky thief who steals your focus and willpower without you even noticing. Every day, you're hit with thousands of choices—what to eat, what to tackle first, how to reply to that email—and each one chips away at your brain's limited mental energy. By afternoon, you're not just worn out; your judgment's shaky, you're procrastinating more, and you're more likely to grab junk food or binge-scroll instead of doing what matters. Judges in a famous study granted parole at 70% early in the day, but only at 10% by late afternoon—not because their cases changed, but because their decision-making capacity was depleted.

## How It Sneaks Up on You

Picture starting your morning strong: coffee, emails sorted, and a big project underway. But then the small stuff piles on—outfit choices, lunch options, meeting agendas. Your prefrontal cortex, the brain's chief executive responsible for focus and self-control, begins to struggle. Science shows it works like a muscle: strong at first, but it fatigues with overuse. Suddenly, the amygdala—the emotional panic button—takes over, sparking impulsive buys, snappy replies, or skipping the gym. We've all been there after a long day, right? Have you ever indulged in a regrettable late-night Amazon spree? This phenomenon is commonly referred to as classical decision fatigue.

## Brain Science, Made Simple

Neurologically, decisions burn glucose fast in the prefrontal cortex. Make too many, and activity drops while emotions ramp up—hello, bad calls. However, there is hope: you can manage it effectively. Sleep, hydration, and even quick mindfulness breaths recharge that executive center. High-achievers get this—Steve Jobs stuck to black turtlenecks daily; Obama limited suits to blue or gray. They saved brainpower for the big stuff, like leading the free world or revolutionizing tech.

## Habits: Your Automatic Shield

Habits are genius because they bypass the whole decision mess. Your basal ganglia handles brushing teeth or your commute on autopilot, with no prefrontal drain. Charles Duhigg nails it in his habit loop: cue → routine → reward. Identify your triggers (such as using your phone during breaks for doomscrolling) and consider replacing them with more positive alternatives, like taking a Michael Phelps had the same pre-swim ritual every Olympics; Murakami writes at 4 AM daily and then runs. Start small—a fixed morning flow: wake, water, plan. Boom, your day flows easier, and decisions lighten up.

## Practical Moves to Beat It

Ready to fight back? Try these—they're simple but game-changing:

- **Hit the big decisions first.** Save willpower peaks for career moves or tough talks; delegate the rest.
- **Two-minute rule.** Tiny choices? Do 'em now so they don't clutter your head.
- **Batch like tasks.** Consolidate emails into one 30-minute block instead of spreading them throughout the day to reduce mental switching costs.
- **Set defaults.** Weekly meal prep, same work outfit, go-to playlist. Fewer options, more energy.
- **Decision-free breaks.** Spending five minutes staring out of a window or deep breathing allows you to make no choices and simply reset.

Daniel Kahneman aptly stated that top decision-makers ruthlessly filter information rather than drowning in it.

## Why It Pays Off Long-Term

Nail this, and it's not just about crushing today—it's compounding wins. Better hires, consistent workouts, and sharper focus week after week. You dodge burnout, feel in control, and actually enjoy your time instead of fighting it. Time management isn't grinding harder; it's designing smarter around your brain's limits.

```
Start tonight: Spot one draining choice tomorrow and
automate it. Watch how freed-up energy snowballs into real
```

progress. You've got this--your sharper self is waiting.

# 25

# The Role of Environment.

"Your environment shapes your behavior more than your willpower ever will. Design it wisely, and time becomes your ally."

The spaces we inhabit—our homes, offices, and even digital landscapes—play a silent yet profound role in how we manage time. Think of your environment as the invisible hand that either nudges you toward productivity or pulls you into procrastination. In this chapter, we'll explore how surroundings influence focus, energy, and efficiency, and how you can engineer your environment to work for you, not against you.

Your surroundings shape your productivity more than you think—it's like your brain's picking up invisible signals from clutter, light, noise, and even smells that either fire you up or drag you down. A messy desk pulls your focus like a magnet, while natural light lifts your mood and sharpens your thinking. Studies show clutter stresses you out and tanks performance, but simple tweaks—like clearing junk or letting in sunlight—can change everything.

## How Your Space Secretly Runs the Show

Think "choice architecture": everything around you nudges your habits. Phone face-down? Fewer distractions. Water bottle right there? You drink more, stay sharper. Even room temp matters—a comfy 77°F makes people type faster and better than chilly offices. Noisy open plans scatter your brain; quiet corners let you dive deep, like Cal Newport's "deep work" setup.

At home, it's tricky—work and chill bleed together. Don't work from bed; your brain mixes rest with stress. Pick a dedicated spot, add calming blues or greens, spritz peppermint for alertness. Tell family your "quiet hours," and stash work gadgets from the bedroom. Plants? They clean air and chill you out.

## Tame Your Digital Jungle

Phones are sneaky thieves—the average person checks 58 times a day, and each ping steals 23 minutes to refocus. Kill notifications, delete junk apps, use blockers like StayFocusd. Clean your desktop, batch emails (two-minute ones? Zap 'em now). Sans-serif fonts speed reading; tools like Notion keep chaos visual and simple.

## Micro-Spaces for Different Vibes

Match spots to tasks: café buzz for brainstorming, library hush for grinding. Instrumental tunes (lo-fi or Baroque) boost focus without lyrics. Stand sometimes to wake up your energy. Keep a "focus kit"—headphones, water, notebook—ready to roll.

## Keep It Fresh

Reset weekly: declutter, tweak what's off. Track what works—if a corner distracts, swap it. Share with roommates for backup. James Clear nails it: you don't rise to goals, you fall to your systems. Treat your space like a teammate, and watch time stretch.

Quick wins to start:

- Clear one shelf today.
- Dim distractions, crank light.
- Test a new "focus corner."

```
Your environment's got your back when you design it
right--small changes, big flow.
```

# 26

# The Power of Accountability.

"Accountability is the glue that ties commitment to results." - Bob Proctor

Accountability is not just a corporate term; it truly transforms the process of completing tasks and maintaining them over time. Research indicates that individuals who have an accountability partner or system are 42% more likely to achieve their goals compared to those who rely solely on their own willpower. It taps into our wiring: when you tell someone your plan—a friend, mentor, or even an app—you feel an electric pull to follow through because backing out feels inconsistent with what you said. Nobody wants that mental itch of letting themselves (or others) down.

Think about the Hawthorne Effect: people just work harder and smarter when they know someone's paying attention. In one old workplace study, output spiked simply because workers felt observed. In your personal life, sharing your goals can lead to a consistent increase in your productivity. Wild stat from the American Society of Training:

odds of success jump from 10% on your own to 95% with a partner holding you accountable. That's huge.

It's not all about outside pressure, though. Tracking your wins, deadlines, and slip-ups in a journal or check-in builds crazy self-awareness. You spot patterns early—like procrastination creeping in—and course-correct before it derails you. Pair that with a quick weekly review, and you're not just disciplined; you're unstoppable. Try declaring one goal to a friend today—you'll feel the difference.

So, how can you harness this power in your daily life? The key lies in **intentional systems**—whether through people, technology, or structured routines. Below, we'll explore the most effective accountability strategies that can transform how you manage time and achieve success.

**Pick Your Accountability Crew Wisely**

Not just anyone works as an accountability partner. You need someone reliable who shows up, gives honest feedback with encouragement, and keeps you on track without killing your vibe. Mastermind groups or daily stand-up check-ins work great—sharing goals publicly (like Elon tweeting deadlines) amps up the pressure to deliver.

**Solo? Try These:**

- **Seinfeld Chain:** X every day you hit your goal. Hate breaking streaks.
- **Time-block + review:** Grade your day, use Toggl to track.
- **Public pledge:** Post a 30-day goal online.

**Quick Start:**

- Find your person/app today

- Set one check-in rule
- Go public with a small goal

Miss a day? No sweat—just don't skip twice. Accountability isn't chains; it's rocket fuel. Who's holding you accountable?

# 27

# The Science of Sprints and Marathons.

Productivity's got two sides—like sprinting vs. marathoning. You can't just grind nonstop; you've got to mix intense bursts with steady pacing to avoid crashing. Alex, a dev buried in deadlines, switched to 90-min focus sprints + 20-min breaks—output up, burnout gone. Science says our brains run on ultradian rhythms (90-120 min cycles), so work with 'em: tackle big stuff in peaks, and walk or chill in dips.

Time blocking is your blueprint—slot tasks like Elon's 5-min chunks or Cal Newport's deep work slabs. Ditch multitasking (it dings IQ 15 points); group emails, and guard buffers. Sarah, the marketer, blocked creative mornings and meeting afternoons—suddenly she owned her day.

Energy's the real fuel. Raj, the founder, ditched 80-hr weeks for workouts, naps, and gratitude—the company thrived. Manage physical (sleep/walks), mental (Pomodoro), emotional (relationships), and spiritual (purpose) aspects. Hustle culture lies—over 50 hrs/week tanks you.

Beware endless sprints: Mia the lawyer burned out at 60+ hrs. Spot fatigue, cynicism? Force rest days, delegate. Playing the long game pays off—Maria wrote daily for years and eventually became a bestseller. James Clear's 1% rule: tiny habits compound.

```
Your moves:
Track your energy week
Block time, start small
Sprint smart, recover hard
Focus process over finish lines
Master sprint-marathon, and time works for you. Pace wins
races.
```

# 28

# The Future of Time Management.

Time management isn't a fixed skill you learn once and forget about—it's constantly changing with the world around us.

New tech, evolving work cultures, and a deeper understanding of how our brains function are all reshaping how we use our time. With AI assistants, smarter apps, and science-backed productivity methods on the rise, the way we plan our days in the future will look very different from today.

In this chapter, we'll look at the trends and tools that are starting to redefine time management—so you're not just keeping up with a fast-paced world, but actually staying a step ahead.

## The Rise of AI-Powered Productivity

rtificial intelligence isn't some distant, sci-fi idea anymore—it's already sitting inside your calendar, inbox, and to-do list, quietly changing how you use your time.

AI tools like smart calendars, virtual assistants, and apps such as Motion or Reclaim.ai can now learn your habits, reshuffle your day, and even protect your focus. They can notice when you work best, suggest time blocks for deep work, and gently push low-value tasks out of your peak hours. In the near future, they'll likely use things like your sleep data or stress levels to plan your day even more precisely.

One of the most powerful shifts is predictive prioritization: instead of you constantly deciding, *"What should I do next?"*, AI can read deadlines, project links, and your energy patterns to build a smart to-do list for you—and keep adjusting it as life happens.

But there's a catch. If we hand over everything to AI, we risk living on autopilot, just following notifications instead of making conscious choices. The sweet spot is partnership, not surrender: let AI do the heavy lifting—tracking, scheduling, nudging—while *you* stay the one who chooses what truly matters.

AI time tracking is also getting sharper. Instead of manually logging hours, systems can tell what you're doing with your apps, emails, and meetings, then show you where your time actually goes. They might soon say things like:

- "You've been in meetings for 3 hours—take a break."
- "You usually focus best between 9–11 AM. Want to block that for deep work?"
- "You've hit 40 minutes of social media—want to cap it for today?"

The future of time management isn't just "work faster." It's smarter, more personal, and more humane—if we use AI as a co-pilot that supports our priorities, not one that quietly replaces them.

## The Science of Chronobiology and Peak Performance

Time management isn't just about *what* you do, it's about *when* you do it. That's where chronobiology—the science of your body clock—comes in. Your energy, focus, and creativity rise and fall in natural rhythms during the day. Most people hit a slump between 2–4 PM. Instead of guzzling coffee and forcing deep work, the future of time management will lean into this: admin, emails, and easy tasks in low-energy hours; deep focus work during your natural peak (usually in 90–120 minute "power blocks").

Wearables like Oura and Whoop are already tracking sleep, stress, and recovery. Soon, they'll talk directly to your calendar—shifting meetings, suggesting focus blocks, and nudging you to rest when your body's showing signs of overload. The goal isn't a rigid bio-robot schedule but flexible days built around your biology, not the old-school 9-to-5.

For years we glorified multitasking. Now we know that it trashes our focus. Your brain doesn't actually do two demanding things at once—it just switches really fast, and that switch costs energy and accuracy. The future belongs to **deep work**: distraction-free blocks where you do one meaningful thing at a time.

Tools will increasingly support that, with things like

- Smart "focus modes" that mute everything non-urgent.
- Automatic Do Not Disturb during your peak focus windows
- Feedback when you're mentally overloaded so you can pause *before* you burn out

Instead of stuffing more into your day, the shift is toward doing fewer things better—with your full attention.

**The Role of Virtual and Augmented Reality in Time Optimization**

Virtual reality (VR) and augmented reality (AR) are also about to mess (in a good way) with how we use time. Imagine slipping on a headset and stepping into your ideal workspace: no clutter, no noise, just a calm virtual studio or boardroom. Imagine wearing AR glasses that discreetly project your to-do list, next steps, or instructions into your field of view as you work.

Do you need to prepare for an important day? VR could let you "rehearse" tomorrow's schedule or presentation in a safe, simulated environment. Of course, with more immersion comes the risk of mental overload, so future time management will likely include intentional "offline time" to let your brain decompress.

## The Shift Toward Outcome-Based Time Management

We are also transitioning from focusing on "How many hours did you work?" to emphasizing "What did you actually accomplish?" That's **outcome-based time management**. Remote work has already proved you don't need to be chained to a desk to be effective. The people and companies that will thrive are the ones who:

- Measure results, not time logged.
- Use tools that show progress and impact, not just busywork
- Regularly ask, "What can I *stop* doing?" as much as "What should I do next?"

Discerning low-impact tasks consciously allows you to focus your time on tasks that truly make a difference.

In the end, the future of time management isn't just more apps, more hacks, or more automation. It's more *intentionality*. Smarter tech, better understanding of our bodies, and new ways of working are giving us a huge opportunity: to design days that fit us—our energy, our values, our goals.

```
Time won't slow down. But how you use it can become far more
human, aligned, and meaningful.
```

# 29

# Conclusion: Crafting Your Masterpiece.

```
"Time isn't just a resource-it's the foundation of a meaningful life. How you spend your minutes determines the legacy you leave behind."
```

## The Art and Science of Time Mastery-

Time is the canvas you're painting your entire life on—and how you use it is both art and science. All through this book, we've discussed ideas, tools, and psychology, but ideas only matter when they show up in your everyday routine. This chapter is your moment to pull it all together and build a time system that actually fits *you*—your goals, your values, and your real life (not the ideal one in your head).

It all starts with self-awareness. Notice your natural rhythm: Are you sharp in the morning or come alive at night? Do long meetings drain you? Do open, unstructured days make you procrastinate? When you understand your energy peaks and common traps, you can plan your day in a way that works *with* your body and brain, not against them.

Then comes the toolkit. Maybe short bursts like the Pomodoro Technique help you start, or maybe you love long, deep-focus sessions. Maybe a digital planner or calendar app keeps you on track, or you feel more connected to your time when you're writing in a notebook or bullet journal. There's no "right" way—just your way. Try things, tweak them, keep what works, and drop what doesn't.

You're not trying to copy someone else's system. You're building your own.

Finally, remember that time mastery isn't about rigid control—it's about flexibility and resilience. Life is unpredictable, and even the best-laid plans can be disrupted. The true test of your system isn't whether you stick to it perfectly, but how quickly and gracefully you adapt when things go off track.

## Designing Your Personalized Time Management System

**Step 1: Check Where Your Time Really Goes**

For one week, write down what you do every 30 minutes. Be specific: instead of "work," write things like "emails," "meeting," "scrolling Instagram," "YouTube," etc.

Then group what you did into:

1. **Essential** – must-do responsibilities
2. **High-value** – things that move you toward your goals

3. **Low-value** – busywork someone else could do
4. **Time wasters** – little or no real benefit

This gives you a clear picture of what to keep, cut, or change.

**Step 2: Use the Eisenhower Matrix**

Not everything is equally important. Sort your tasks into:

- **Urgent & Important** → Do now
- **Important, Not Urgent** → Schedule time for them
- **Urgent, Not Important** → Delegate if you can
- **Not Urgent, Not Important** → Reduce or remove

This helps you stop living in "firefighting mode" and focus on what truly matters.

**Step 3: Block Time for Deep Work**

Pick 60–90-minute blocks for important, brain-heavy work. During these blocks:

- Turn off notifications
- Close extra tabs
- Let people know you're not available

Protect this time like an appointment with your future self.

**Step 4: Automate, Delegate, Eliminate (ADE)**

Free up your time by:

1. **Automating** – bills, reminders, email filters, templates
2. **Delegating** – tasks others can do 70–80% as well as you

3. **Eliminating** – stuff that doesn't support your goals

If it doesn't matter, it doesn't deserve your time.

**Step 5: Do a Weekly Review**

Once a week, take 10–15 minutes to ask:

- What worked well?
- What didn't?
- Where did I waste time?
- What will I change next week?

Adjust a little each week, and your system will keep getting better.

## Overcoming Common Time Management Pitfalls

### *The Myth of Multitasking*

Many people pride themselves on juggling multiple tasks at once, but research shows that multitasking reduces productivity by up to 40%. Your brain isn't wired to focus on several things simultaneously—instead, it rapidly switches between tasks, leading to mental fatigue and errors.

### *Perfectionism Paralysis*

Striving for excellence is admirable, but perfectionism can be a trap. When you obsess over every detail, you waste time on diminishing returns. Adopt the **80/20 Rule**: 80% of results come from 20% of effort. Focus on "good enough" and ship your work.

### *The Planning Fallacy*

Humans consistently underestimate how long tasks will take. Combat this by:

1. Breaking projects into smaller steps.
2. Adding a 20% buffer to time estimates.
3. Reflecting on past tasks to improve future predictions.

### *Decision Fatigue*

Every choice you make depletes mental energy. Reduce decision fatigue by:

- Creating routines (e.g., morning rituals, meal prepping).
- Limiting trivial decisions (e.g., wearing a "uniform" to save brain-

power).

- Batching similar tasks (e.g., answering emails in one sitting).

### *The "Busy" Trap*

Being busy doesn't equal being productive. Avoid glorifying busyness by regularly asking, *"Is this activity moving me closer to my goals?"*

## Sustaining Long-Term Success

### *Cultivating Discipline Over Motivation*

Motivation is fleeting; discipline is what carries you through. Build habits that make productivity automatic:

**Start with small, manageable changes.**

Use habit stacking (e.g., "After my morning coffee, I'll review my priorities").

Track progress to stay accountable.

**The Power of Reflection**

Regular reflection reinforces growth. Set aside monthly time for:

1. Celebrate wins (no matter how small).
2. Analyze setbacks without self-judgment.

3. Adjust strategies for the coming month.

**Embracing Rest as a Productivity Tool**

Burnout is the enemy of sustained success. Schedule downtime just as rigorously as work blocks. Remember:

```
"Rest is not the opposite of productivity-it's the
foundation of it."
```

## Your Time Mastery Action Plan

Now, it's time to put everything into practice. Here's your step-by-step action plan:

1. Conduct a time audit (Track your activities for a week).
2. Define Your Priorities (Use the Eisenhower Matrix).
3. Design Your Ideal Week (Block time for deep work, rest, and reflection).
4. Implement the ADE Method (Automate, Delegate, Eliminate).
5. Review Weekly (Adjust and refine your system).

By following this framework, you'll transform time-stressed chaos into a life of purpose, productivity, and fulfillment. The masterpiece of your life is waiting—now, go craft it, one minute at a time.

# About the Author

Vivek Kumar is a lifelong learner who believes books can quietly change a person's entire direction in life. As a sales and marketing professional for over 20 years, he spent countless hours in meetings, targets, and travel—yet always carried a book in his bag and a question in his mind: "How can these ideas reach everyday people in a simple, usable way?"

That question led him to create the *Book Reading Marathon: The Read and Rise Challenge*, a 52-week experiment where readers don't just finish books, they apply them—one small habit, one tiny shift at a time. Out of this journey came Spark-loom ideas , along with his earlier works: *The Magic of Never Surrender, Think Different, Win Big, Words Magical Power, StickWise habits, Mindshift Odyssey , Productively Productive, JoyMap Blueprint and Spart-Loom ideas.*

Vivek's style is practical and down-to-earth. He doesn't write as a distant expert but as someone walking the same path—balancing work, family, dreams, and doubts—while using books as tools to build a better inner world. Through his writing, talks, and online community, he aims to make personal growth feel less overwhelming and more like a friendly conversation that nudges you to take your next small, brave step.

# Also by Vivek Kumar

**Read 52 Self-Help Books in 52 Weeks: Book Reading Marathon: The Read and Rise Challenge.**

Read 52 Self-Help Books in 52 Weeks: The Book Reading Marathon Challenge is your step-by-step guide to building the life-changing habit of reading and applying the wisdom of the world's greatest self-help books.

This book introduces you to the Book Reading Marathon: The Read and Rise Challenge—a structured program where readers commit to finishing one self-help book every week for a year. Instead of simply collecting books or reading randomly, this challenge follows a planned sequence of seven powerful themes: 1️⃣Habits

2️⃣Mindset

3️⃣Productivity

4️⃣Creativity

5️⃣Time Management

6️⃣Positive Psychology

7️⃣Leadership

Each series contains seven handpicked books, making it easier for readers to dive deep into every theme while maintaining balance and variety.

Inside this book, you will discover:

Why reading self-help books consistently can transform your career, relationships, and personal growth.

Practical tools: summaries, key insights, and frameworks that help you grasp the core lessons of each book with clarity and ease.

**Words' Magical Power: Words That Win.**

Unlock the hidden power of language with *Words' Magical Power: Words That Win.* In this insightful book, Vivek Kumar reveals how the words we choose can shape our reality, influence others, and determine our success. Drawing from psychology and practical communication strategies, this book guides you to speak with confidence, persuade with clarity, and create positive impact in both personal and professional life. Whether you want to improve your conversations, presentations, or mindset, this book unlocks the magic behind words that truly win.

**The Magic of Never Surrender.**

In a world of challenges and uncertainties, the journey from student to leader is often fraught with obstacles, setbacks, and moments of doubt. However, these moments of adversity sow the seeds of resilience, determination, and unwavering commitment to one's dreams.

"The Magic Of Never Surrender: Defying the Odds and Achieving Greatness" is more than just a book; it is a guiding light for those navigating the tumultuous waters of personal and professional growth. Through the pages of this insightful and empowering work, readers embark on a transformative journey fueled by the unwavering belief that no obstacle is insurmountable and no dream is beyond reach.

Drawing upon personal experiences, anecdotes, and lessons learned from the trenches of academia and the boardroom, the author offers a compelling road map for overcoming adversity, embracing failure as a stepping stone to success, and cultivating the mindset of a true leader. From the importance of resilience in the face of adversity to the power of perseverance in pursuit of one's dreams, each chapter is a poignant reminder of the boundless potential within each of us.

Through practical strategies, actionable insights, and thought-provoking reflections, "The Magic Of Never Surrender" equips readers with the tools and mindset needed to navigate the complexities of the modern world with confidence, courage, and resilience. Whether you are a student embarking on the journey of self-discovery or a seasoned professional navigating the challenges of leadership, this book serves as a beacon of hope and inspiration, illuminating the path toward personal and professional fulfillment.

As you move on this transformative journey, I encourage you to embrace the wisdom within these pages with an open heart and a steadfast determination to never give up on your dreams. True leaders are forged through perseverance, resilience, and fierce loyalty, leaving an indelible mark on the world and inspiring others to follow in their footsteps.

May "The Magic Of Never Surrender: Defying the Odds and Achieving Greatness" be your companion and guide on realizing your fullest potential and achieving your wildest dreams. Remember, the journey may be challenging, but with perseverance, determination, and an unwavering belief in yourself, success is not just a possibility—it is inevitable.

**Think Different, Win Big.**

What if the key to your success lies not in hard work but in thinking differently? In "Think Different, Win Big: The Power of Strategic Mind Shifts," Vivek Kumar reveals the transformative power of a new mindset, drawing from nearly two decades of experience in sales and marketing. This book is not just a guide but a roadmap to transcending mediocrity and seizing extraordinary opportunities through the mastery of strategic thinking.

Kumar's insights challenge conventional wisdom, demonstrating that success begins in the mind. Real-world successes support his expertise, which he forged in the competitive arenas of sales and marketing. Through engaging narratives and practical wisdom, Kumar empowers readers to pivot in the face of adversity, transforming challenges into opportunities.

Are you ready to unlock your true potential and redefine your reality? Dive into "Think Different, Win Big" and discover the power of strategic mind shifts. The adventure starts now.

**Leadership Simplified.**

**Leadership Simplified: A Quick Guide to Effective Leadership"**

**It is a transformative handbook that navigates the complex world of leadership with clarity and purpose. Whether you are a seasoned manager seeking to enhance your skills or a budding leader eager to make your mark, this book offers a concise and insightful exploration of the key principles that distinguish exceptional leaders from the rest.**

At the core of this guide is a thought-provoking question: What separates an average manager from an exceptional leader? The chapters unfold a systematic journey, exploring the depths of leadership through real-life examples, case studies, and practical strategies. From understanding the leader within to mastering the power of influence, leading with vision, and empowering others, each chapter provides actionable insights to unlock your full leadership potential.

The book recognizes the importance of simplicity in leadership, emphasizing that effective leadership is not about complexity but about clarity. It is a compass guiding readers through self-awareness, influential communication, visionary thinking, and resilience in challenging times.

With a heartfelt dedication to mentors who have shaped the author's own leadership journey, "Leadership Simplified" stands as a testament to the transformative impact of guidance and mentorship. This quick guide is more than just a book; it is an invitation to embark on a lifelong journey of growth, inspiration, and effective leadership.

Are you ready to simplify the complex world of leadership and unlock your true leadership potential? Dive into "Leadership Simplified" and discover the keys to becoming the exceptional leader you are meant to be.

**MINDSHIFT ODYSSEY.**

Mindshift Odyssey distills that fire into your hands—not as abstract theory, but as a 21-day transformation blueprint. From crushing limiting beliefs to forging grit, supercharging learning, and crafting an impossible dream statement, every chapter packs exercises born from my experiments in content creation and personal reinvention. This is Book 2 in the series, building on the mindset foundations to propel you toward lasting change.

**JoyMap Blueprint: A Practical Guide to Everyday Happiness.** Joy isn't a mystery—it's a map.

And this book is your map.

**JoyMap Blueprint: A Practical Guide to Everyday Happiness** shows you how to design a life where happiness isn't something you chase someday, but something you experience every single day. Blending science, stories, and simple exercises, Vivek Kumar breaks big ideas about positive psychology into small, doable steps you can actually follow in real life. Book 4 BRMC CCC

Drawing on timeless happiness classics like *The Happiness Advantage, Flourish, The How of Happiness, The Gifts of Imperfection, The Art of Happiness, Learned Optimism,* and *Authentic Happiness,* this book turns research into routines you can plug straight into your mornings, workdays, and relationships. You'll explore everything from gratitude, small wins, resilience, and mindset to habits, health, money, simplicity, play, and purpose—then pull it all together into your personal "JoyMap" for the long term.

Inside, you'll learn how to:

**Understand the science of happiness—and actually use it**

**Spot and multiply "micro-joys" in ordinary days**

**Bounce forward from setbacks with practical resilience tools**

**Design ideal days that match your values, energy, and goals**

**Build positive habits that stick (without relying on willpower)**

**Create a JoyMap that's uniquely yours—and easy to sustain**

Whether you're feeling a little stuck, quietly "fine" but not fulfilled, or already on a growth journey and ready for your next level, **JoyMap Blueprint** gives you a friendly, structured way to upgrade your inner world and outer life—one small, joyful step at a time.